THE HEALING FIELD

THE HEALING FIELD

Exceptional Healing Practices To Change Your Life

PENNY PRICE LAVIN

iUniverse®

THE HEALING FIELD
Exceptional Healing Practices To Change Your Life

iUniverse books may be ordered through booksellers or by contacting:

iUniverse
1663 Liberty Drive
Bloomington, IN 47403
www.iuniverse.com
1-800-Authors (1-800-288-4677)

ISBN: 978-1-5320-9239-8 (sc)
ISBN: 978-1-5320-9238-1 (e)

Library of Congress Control Number: 2020900401

Print information available on the last page.

iUniverse rev. date: 03/09/2020

Book Reviews For

THE HEALING FIELD:

Exceptional Healing Practices to Change Your Life

The book is based on the Telly-winning film of the same name. The film was honored at the Woodstock Museum Film Festival.

"A well-documented and credible voice that not only challenges the paradigms of Western biomedicine, but also offers detailed maps of many of the major healing modalities emerging in our time. If you are trying to make sense out of the contemporary health and healing scene, this is a superb resource."- Rick Jarow, author, *Creating the Work You Love,* and *In Search of the Sacred.*

"Penny Price Lavin has brought together renowned experts in the role of consciousness and energy healing to create a comprehensive and inspiring overview of the subject. Integrating scientific knowledge with traditional wisdom, this book is a must for anyone interested in the alternative approaches to health."- Peter Russell, author, *The Global Brain* and *From Science to God.*

"An important contribution to helping us understand how holistic healing practices reawaken our consciousness, humanity, and oneness." — Karen D. Saroop, *The Green Brain Initiative*

"I love your informative book, *The Healing Field.* It is powerful and inclusive and is helping to bring all this work forward. I think times are changing and energy healing will be the new health care. Allopathic will be the secondary healing. It may not happen in our life-time, but I am certain that it is moving in that direction. There are so many modalities that can help with our healing that have nothing to do with popping a prescribed allopathic drug."- Nancy McAlley, RN, Energy Healer and Homeopathic student

"This is one of the best books I have seen concerning biofield therapy and energy medicine. The simple explanations and examples are so easy to understand. The experts are physicists and well-known experts in the science of energy medicine. This work makes real something I have long believed to be a necessary part of our Western medical practices." – Linnie Thomas, HTCI (Healing Touch Certified Instructor)

"*The Healing Field* is a deeply meaningful and informative film and book. I'm so grateful that it has been made into a book, because it presents the kind of material that needs to be seen and read over and over again because of the depth of the message. I especially enjoyed the ending in Part 1, where it calls for unity. Transforming the self, transforming the world."- Joan Baird, LCSW-R (Licensed Clinical Social Worker)

"*The Healing Field* is FABULOUS!!! I especially love how the experts give the scientific evidence for energy healing in a language that we who are not scientists can clearly understand!" - Mary Kay McGraw, LMT (Licensed Massage Therapist)

"I am proud to be a participant in *The Healing Field*! Penny Price Lavin has done a magnificent job of describing how human beings share an interconnectedness with each other and the greater Universe. The work evokes a palpable sense of healing in the viewer and the reader, raising us to a higher, more integrated state both within ourselves, with each other, and with All That Is. You will be transformed." - Hyla Cass MD, author, *8 Weeks to Vibrant Health*

"I'm very proud and honored to be a part of *The Healing Field.* I love it! I've gotten positive feedback from everyone who has seen the film and read the book. Thank you again."- Gary Renza, Qigong Master

CONTENTS

WITH GRATITUDE

My deepest appreciation and gratitude goes to all the exceptional experts and practitioners who shared their brilliant expertise and generous hearts, and contributed to my documentary and this book. See Acknowledgments for their detailed information.

Special thanks to integrative medicine experts Hyla Cass, MD, and Larry Dossey, MD; Bruce Lipton, PhD, cell biologist; Rollin McCraty, PhD, from Heartmath; Lynne McTaggart, consciousness expert; the late Candace Pert, PhD, neuroscientist; Beverly Rubik, PhD, biophysicist;

And energy practitioners and experts, Ron Lavin, MA, founder and director of *One Light Healing Touch*; Linnie Thomas, HTCI from *Healing Touch*; Qigong Masters, Kenneth Cohen, Jack Lim, and Gary Renza; Mental Imagery Experts, Rachel Epstein and Gerald Epstein, MD; and sound healing experts Melodee Gabler and Philippe Garnier. I also thank the media platforms Beyond Words and Gaia.com for their kindness and support of the documentary, *The Healing Field;* and to my husband, Ron Lavin, for his wisdom, humor, support and shining inspiration in life and in the field of energy healing; and to Judith Oringer for her assistance editing the book.

PREFACE

My life path has always been ignited by the desire to bring in light and healing, both in the media and in healing work. I have been spiritually attuned since childhood, when I first began to sense a deep, inner spiritual connection. I recount those stories in the section, *About the Author*. In my media career I have been particularly motivated by topics that promote self-empowerment, personal transformation and healing, particularly in the areas of wellness and spirituality.

I have been fortunate to work on many respected national television programs, including, *The Mike Douglas Show, Good Morning America, NBC Magazine, Kids Are People Too*, and *Geraldo,* where I have received Maggie and Emmy Awards and peer recognition for my programs on AIDS and the environment.

My life and career went through a pivotal shift when I moved to Los Angeles and served as a studio executive and freelance producer. During this time, I also learned Reiki, a popular energy healing method. When I practiced on friends, I experienced an unshakable feeling that I was connecting to something ancient, that I had done this before! A few years later, I met my remarkable husband, Ron Lavin, a gifted psychic and energy healer, who taught me his energy healing method, One Light Healing Touch. I was in love with both my husband and energy healing, and I became an enthusiastic practitioner and developed an active healing practice. Over the years, I became an Instructor and taught workshops on energy healing in New York City, the Hudson Valley, Los Angeles and Orlando.

Later, I left mainstream television and decided to form my own production company, Penny Price Media, so I could devote all my energies to producing body, mind and spirit programs, many of which have received film festival awards, acclaimed reviews, and have aired on PBS.

As I surveyed the media landscape, I saw that the public had minimal understanding of energy medicine and was not aware that it could help them improve their lives - body, mind and spirit. I felt a deep inner yearning to bring light, education and understanding and help remedy that gap. The result is my Telly-winning documentary, *The Healing Field – Exploring Energy & Consciousness,* which can now be seen in many foreign countries and has been well-received by experts and thousands of lay energy practitioners alike.

The film features renowned experts who present enlightening breakthroughs and explain how our health, body and awareness are influenced by our mind, emotions and consciousness. In addition, the film features cutting-edge energy healing and mind-body practitioners who share compelling information and numerous methods for self-healing.

I wanted to write this book for several reasons. People around the world continually write to me, saying that the film should be watched over and over again, because the material is both deep and highly relevant. Now with this book, readers can do just that, and they can re-read it as often as they wish! Second, I wanted to give the readers more extensive information on all the topics covered in the film, from in-depth expert material, to proven excellent energy and mind-body techniques. Third, with the rising costs of health care, we can all benefit from learning simple, self-care tools to help us attain optimum health.

I consider this book a health tool both for individuals and for our society.

Personal growth begins with conscious awareness to identify what is in disharmony in our lives. We all need to learn effective tools to help us regain our balance, attain better health and inner peace and help us open to "our better angels." I suggest that the best entry point is to learn the invaluable practice of meditation. It expands our awareness, connects us to our heart, reduces stress and pain, and allows us to hear our own inner guidance.

Interestingly enough, in the last century various spiritual teachers have prophesied that the next era would see a worldwide increase in people opening to their intuition and practicing energy healing work. Indeed, the world needs to utilize these skills now more than ever before! The world is more chaotic and out of balance, and energy healing and the many practices offered in this book can help us to regain our balance, improve our health, deepen our spiritual awareness and expand our consciousness.

INTRODUCTION

Many people are sensing a global awakening, toward a sense of oneness, and energy medicine and mind/body practitioners are being called to participate. I strongly believe that when we learn to use these remarkable practices and mind-body techniques on a daily basis, from energy healing, Qigong, sound healing, mental imagery, yoga, and meditation, to name a few, we connect with our world in a deeper, more meaningful way, and can better help contribute to humanity's evolution.

This book is based on my documentary, ***The Healing Field - Exploring Energy & Consciousness.*** It includes interviews from the documentary, and it also presents compelling new interviews and material with notable practitioners in these fields. Brilliant experts present fascinating information on energy medicine, which will enhance your understanding of energy, health and the inner workings of consciousness.

The Chapters 1-6 mark the documentary's sections including:

- How medicine is changing
- Genetics - Genes and the environment
- Energy fields
- New frontiers of medicine
- The biochemistry of emotions
- How our heart and mind affect our health and the importance of self care.

Chapters 7-11: These chapters present a range of respected practitioners from the fields of Energy Healing, Qigong, Mental Imagery and Sound Healing. Each chapter explores their work and presents inspiring personal healing stories.

Chapter 7 Energy Healing: One Light Healing Touch™ an International Energy Healing and Mystery School with Ron Lavin, MA. This offers a rare look at a respected training program for people seeking personal healing or to become energy practitioners. It also includes Ron Lavin's and Instructors' healing stories. We also explore A Healing Touch™ an energy healing method popular with nurses that conducts extensive studies in the field.

Chapter 8 Qigong: Rich details about its history and healing stories. Renowned experts explain that our very existence depends on the strength of our Chi energy.

Chapter 9 Mental Imagery: Fascinating information on mental imagery and memorable healing stories. Discover the secrets of miraculous healing with mental imagery by using micro input for macro output.

Chapter 10 Sound Healing: Practitioners from around the world share insights and healing stories. Learn the mysteries of Sound Healing for helping to heal disease.

Chapter 11: Self-Healing Practices are presented in clear detail to help our readers of any age, or any level of ability, learn the work for their own self care and self-empowerment. This includes practices from One Light Healing Touch; Qigong; Mental Imagery, Heartmath, and Sound Work.

Chapter 12: A Summary. Inspiring experts share their thoughts about our evolution, consciousness and the future of energy medicine.

Chapter 13: Studies in the fields of Energy Healing, Qigong, Mental Imagery and Sound Healing.

Chapter 14: Ron Lavin shares his remarkable story of being born a psychic; and Ron and Penny's spiritually guided love story.

Chapter 15: One Light Healing Touch - An in-depth look, and practitioners' healing stories.

Chapter 16: Supplemental Expert Material: This includes treasures of wisdom from the experts seen in the 82 minute documentary, and those whose interviews did not appear in the film.

- The next sections include: Endnotes; Acknowledgments; Resources and Appendix
- The final section is About the Author, Penny Lavin.

It is my hope that this compelling information on energy medicine will enhance your understanding of health and consciousness. This book will also give readers a plethora of energy and mind-body practices, many time-tested over thousands of years, which can help improve one's health, well-being and happiness.

Please consider this book as a key self-healing tool on your personal path toward wellness, personal freedom and self-empowerment. We can all learn to practice these simple methods on a life-long basis, whatever our age or background. Enjoy!

CHAPTER 1

MEDICINE – THE OLD AND THE NEW (1)

We live in extraordinary times. Advances in science, medicine and consciousness are happening at an accelerating rate. And in the field of health care, the old conventional model relying on surgery and prescription drugs is being challenged by a wave of dramatic, non-invasive energy-based techniques. While many of these techniques are actually centuries old, and are considered controversial by many in mainstream western medicine, they are generating worldwide studies with remarkable results. We'll explore how this fascinating field affects our health, our society and our future.

BRUCE LIPTON, PHD, Cell Biologist

Pre-eminent scientist in the field of quantum physics, DNA and stem cell biology. Bruce is the winner of the 2009 Goi Peace Award. Established in Japan in 2000, which is awarded to individuals for their outstanding contributions toward world peace and harmony. He has written two books, *Spontaneous Evolution* and the bestseller, *The Biology of Belief.*

"In today's world of health care there are two different models of how the human biology works. One of them is based on the physical reality that everything in the universe is made out of matter, and this is a Newtonian view that conventional medicine works with. The view basically says that the body is a machine, it's made out of chemicals, and genes, and if there's anything wrong with the machine, you actually adjust the chemicals and genes as the primary source of the problem.

Another view is based on quantum physics that says that the universe is actually made of our energy and everything that we see as matter is itself actually energy. The significance of the difference between the two is that the invisible forces play a primary role in the new understanding of biology. The new energy medicine and energy become entangled, meaning everything that's made out of energy becomes entangled–you can't separate it.

So that says when we're looking at an individual's life we're not looking just at their physical body, we're looking at their health in regard to what their perceptions in the world are, their family relationships, their job relationships, the world issues at that moment because everything impinges upon our health."

BEVERLY RUBIK, PHD., Biophysicist

Biophysicist and the President of the Institute for Frontier Science in San Francisco. She is renowned for her exploration of and countless studies concerning energy medicine.

"The old medicine is not helping us during this era where chronic degenerative disease is the major culprit. Conventional medicine is perfect for things such as trauma or infectious diseases but very limited in terms of dealing with our chronic illnesses such as diabetes, cancer and heart disease. It's also unsustainable, much too costly, and is often not helping people, and they're getting horrendous side effects. In fact, one of the number one causes of death is death by medicine, which includes side effects and mistakes. So we drastically need something bigger and better. One of the exciting changes in the new health care is that enhanced self-care moves to the forefront."

LYNNE MCTAGGART, Consciousness Expert
Preeminent spokesperson on consciousness and the new physics. Lynne is an award-winning author of six books, including the bestsellers, *The Field* and *The Intention Experiment.*

"The new medicine is all about looking at the body as a dynamic system and understanding that if you affect one part of the body, you affect the rest of it. You put medicine on your arm and you create changes in your leg, in your liver, everywhere. So the new approach is to approach the body as a holistic system and also an energy system. And so we don't have to do things grossly to our physicality, we can treat ourselves through energy and things that we can't really see."

LINNIE THOMAS, HTCI, Healing Touch Practitioner
Healing Touch Instructor and author of the popular book, *The Encyclopedia of Energy Medicine*.

"Energy medicine has been around for many, many thousands of years. But for written documentation we go to the Chinese who started documenting it about 5,000 years ago. There are many reasons why energy medicine is becoming so popular. It's effective, it's gentle, it's non-invasive, and it doesn't have side effects. About 55% of the population now is using alternative medicine and integrative medicine because they're getting results and it's a lot cheaper then going to a doctor."

THE LATE CANDICE PERT, PHD., Neuroscientist
Internationally recognized neuroscientist and pharmacologist, and an expert in mind-body medicine and author of *The Molecules of Emotion.*

"In the history of medicine, mind, emotion, and spirit were completely left out. This is the Western mainstream medicine, as we know it. This came from a silly thing from when Descartes was given the dead bodies by the Pope to work on. So everything about mainstream medicine is sort of lifeless. What's happening now and what's so exciting is to incorporate the new paradigm ideas into medicine, not just that mind matters, but that mind is rather central to our health and to our disease."

LARRY DOSSEY, MD. Integrative Medicine expert
Integrative Medicine expert and author of 11 books, including the bestsellers, *Healing Words, The Power of Prayer* and *The Practice of Medicine*. He is the former Executive Editor at the *Journal of Alternative Therapies in Health and Medicine*.

"There's a good case to be made for spirituality returning to modern medicine.

Currently, there are around 90 medical schools that have developed formal courses that look at the impact of spirituality on health and longevity. The data shows that people who practice some kind of spirituality have a lower instance of all the major diseases, including heart disease and cancer, and they live on average seven to thirteen years longer than people that don't follow a spiritual path.

In addition, these days you cannot get an MD degree from a reputable certified medical school in this country unless you know how to take what's called a spiritual history, where you have to be able to demonstrate that you understand the role of spirituality and delivering compassionate care to sick people. I think we're on the verge of a huge transformation from conventional medicine to health care that involves self-care."

This new understanding in health care shows that people's choices and consciousness matter. Emotions, feelings, attitudes, and choices are huge influences on our diseases and health. In the medical community, this is a radical re-thinking of where most disease comes from.

LYNNE MCTAGGART, Consciousness Expert

"Probably since Newton and Descartes, when magic and mysticism were ripped out of our lives, there has been an enormous separation between science and religion. However, with the discoveries made since Einstein and the advent of Quantum physics, we've understood that the world is very different from what we've been told. And that it is much closer to what the ancients described. There is magic, there is connection between all things."

CHAPTER 2

EPIGENETICS: GENES AND THE ENVIRONMENT (1)

While many scientific advances in the future will undoubtedly be created from gene editing, breakthrough research now shows that our health is not dictated by our genetic blueprints after all.

BRUCE LIPTON, PHD, Cell Biologist
"Today's views of genetics have completely changed. The old view I trained in and taught medical students was a view called genetic determinism and this is the belief that the genes control your traits. It's not just your traits that are structural but also that your physical, emotional, and behavioral traits are as well, so that our lives are a printout of our genetic lineage.

There's a new science today called epigenetics, which is the study of how our cells and our body is affected and controlled by our environment. I first saw the nature of epigenetics 40 years ago when I was culturing stem cells. I had genetically identical cells in three dishes but changed the environment in each dish. In one dish they formed muscle, in another dish the cells formed bone, and in the third dish they formed fat cells. The important point was that all the cells were genetically identical, but their fates were controlled by the environment. Today, this new understanding of environmental control over genes is called epigenetic control."

LYNNE MCTAGGART, Consciousness Expert

"We are now understanding that the membrane of a cell is semi-permeable and there are a lot of protein gatekeeper receptors that let information in or out. Everything in our environment: our diet, the air we breathe, the emotions we hold, the sum total of how we live our lives affects whether a gene gets turned on or off. This is profound because it completely contradicts Darwinian genetics that says, "We are driven by our genes."

How can that be if one little environmental thing like a vitamin can derail all of your genetic history? So scientists are now looking at cancer and all kinds of things from the epi genome and understanding that really, we are getting constructed in a sense from outside in, not inside out as we thought."

BRUCE LIPTON, PHD. Cell Biologist

"The fate of our cells is controlled by the chemistry of our blood and the chemistry of our blood is adjusted by the way we perceive life. If we open our eyes and see love in our presence, we release chemistry in the blood such as oxytocin, dopamine, serotonin, and these chemicals promote health and vitality of the system. In contrast however, if we open our eyes and see something that threatens or scares us, we release a completely different set of chemicals into our blood such as stress hormones and histamine. The difference is these chemicals actually shut down our growth and prepare us for protection.

So it becomes very critical on how we see the world because our perceptions are converted into chemistry and the chemistry directly controls not just our behavior but our genetic expression as well." We live in a vast energy field and peaceful, loving energy environments produce a vastly different affect on us, than a toxic environment. Conversely, whatever energy we feel and emanate, be it kind and peaceful energy, or angry and resentful, creates a powerful affect on us, and those around us.

Our consciousness is the key to bringing our awareness to the present moment. As we become aware of how we are feeling in various environments, we can endeavor to spend less time in toxic environments and also learn to transform and release disruptive energies, through self-healing practices. This will help improve our health, bring balance to our mind and spirit and contribute a more positive energy to our environment.

CHAPTER 3

THE BIOFIELD (1)

As we learn that our genes can actually be turned on and off, not just with drugs, supplements and food, but also by our attitudes, scientific pioneers are now exploring how our non-physical energy field interacts with our health. They call our field, *the Biofield.*

BEVERLY RUBIK, PHD, Biophysicist
"The notion that layers of subtle energies radiate from our bodies is based on ancient Indian thinking and ancient Oriental medicine."

LYNNE MCTAGGART, Consciousness Expert
"Throughout the ages, mystics have talked about the source, the matrix, some sort of all-encompassing field but now, since the advent of quantum physics we've understood that there is a quantum field and physicists are able to do a number of types of experiments to demonstrate and actually measure what's happening in this field."

BRUCE LIPTON, PHD, Cell Biologist
"There's a new understanding in the relationship of matter and energy based on quantum physics. The nature of energy healing that is different from mechanical healing is that energy involves

invisible waves that include thought and what physicists call 'the field.' The field is a whole collection of all the energy that makes up the universe, and it turns out that the field is what shapes matter." As Einstein once remarked 'The field is the sole governing agency of a particle.' What he was talking about is that the invisible forces are primary in shaping the physical world."

The key point is to realize that while energy is unseen it is nevertheless vital and real. We are all affected by the energy field around us, and we are also constantly affecting and changing the field with the thoughts and emotions we radiate.

BEVERLY RUBIK, PHD. Biophysicist
"The biofield is an organizing field within and around the human body or any living thing. It's subtle and very complex in that it consists of many types of fields that we already know about: electromagnetic fields, bio photons, or very low-level particles of light, infrared emission, the brain waves and heart waves."

LYNNE MCTAGGART, Consciousness Expert
"Several decades ago the German physicist, Fritz Albert Pop accidentally discovered that there is light coming out of all living things. He found that all living things send out a tiny current of light. He called it bio photon emissions and found that this light is generated in DNA and acts as a kind of global signaling for the entire body. It's also a communication system with the outside world.

We find that when somebody is ill and you apply medicine to one part of the body, the light doesn't just change there, it changes around the whole body. This is an extraordinary discovery because it demonstrates that the real orchestrator of the body isn't genes or genetic code, it's light."

BEVERLY RUBIK, PHD, Biophysicist
"We are actually radiating like stars at a very low level of light out into the universe and as a result we cannot put a boundary on one person's biofield, and say your biofield stops here and another one starts over there. In some ways we're actually all entangled in this web of life energy. The earth also has some dominant frequencies in its energy field, one of which is called the Shuman resonance, which is about 7.8 hertz."

The Shuman resonance is the very pulse of the Earth at 7.8 hertz, the frequency of Earth's natural harmonies. It is the natural resonant frequency of the planet and matches that of human consciousness at the optimal alpha brain waves.

"This is very interesting because one of the main frequencies that is radiating from our brains when we're very relaxed is about 8 hertz. So I don't think we can clearly distinguish any separation between the fields of life and the fields of earth and cosmos. We're all part of one rich living universe."

CHAPTER 4

NEW FRONTIERS: A FIELD-BASED MODEL OF MEDICINE (1)

Because of these discoveries in quantum physics some experts are calling for a revolutionary new field-based view of medicine and the human body.

BRUCE LIPTON, PHD, Cell Biologist
"There's a radical evolution in health care and it's brought about by new modalities that emphasize energy and vibration."

LYNNE MCTAGGART, Consciousness Expert
"Einstein said, 'The field is the only reality.' It's a brilliant phrase because it really encapsulates what things in the universe actually are. We think of all of us and all things as discreet objects, but actually we're all part of a giant quantum energy field."

BEVERLY RUBIK, PHD, Biophysicist
"In energy medicine we regard the body not just as a bag of molecules, but as primary fields of information that can be shifted by different therapeutics. Things like homeopathy or energy healers or devices can emit certain frequencies that can shift the biofield. And by shifting the biofield, we shift the

dynamics of the body toward a movement toward health and wellness."

BRUCE LIPTON, PHD, Cell Biologist

"We find that atoms aren't physical themselves. They're actually energy vortices. They're like little miniature tornados. Every atom is actually a vibrational field. The significance of this is that when we look at the body through the new scan system such as PET scan, Cat scans, and MRI scans, we're actually looking at the energy profiles of our bodies, not the physical expression of it.

The significance in healing is that in quantum physics the energy can be adjusted by other energy rather then chemistry, and research has now revealed that energy information signals are 100 times more efficient in controlling biology then our chemical signals.

The net result is we will move away from the pharmaceutical pursuit of healing and move into the energy field as a much more effective and efficient way of introducing health into our body."

New frontiers in medicine will explore using many types of energy on the body, from energy healers, homeopathy, acupuncture, to machines using magnetic, electricity and lasers, to seeing the affects of group energy on a common goal. It will no doubt bring a myriad of breakthroughs to the health care field.

CHAPTER 5

THE BIOCHEMISTRY OF OUR EMOTIONS (1)

Along with the remarkable discoveries about the biofield and genetic behavior, one of the most extraordinary new areas of research focuses on how our emotions affect our health and consciousness. The late Candace Pert, PhD. was one of the leading pioneers in this field. She was the author of the groundbreaking book, *The Molecules of Emotions.*

CANDACE PERT, PHD., Neuroscientist

"The primary purpose of the molecules of emotions is to regenerate our body-minds. Every time we think, every time we emote, we are moving cells and we are growing cells.

We are changing the fabric of our body with every thought. Every thought is changing our emotions, and every emotional expression is re-wiring our brain.

The emotions are the key because they're in the physical realm in the forms of these molecules of emotions. But they're also in this mysterious energetic realm. The key is that they are carrying information to a synapse less then a millimeter away or they can carry information all over the body. But when you have a profound emotional trigger, every single receptor in your body shifts so that emotion is felt all over the body-mind.

What we're thinking, what we tend to think, how we hold our muscles, where they are, our whole structure is defined by our emotional state."

BEVERLY RUBIK, PHD., Biophysicist

"Negative thinking along with negative emotions, fears, anxiety, feeling stressed which is most people's constant state, really impacts our organs. It removes blood flow from all the vital organs of our bodies from our stomachs, our hearts, our brains, and it puts blood flow in our muscles and so we're ready for 'fight or flight.'

When people bring positive energy and positive feelings back into their body, their blood flows back to the vital organs and tissues. This allows for all the benefits of the blood, bringing in nutrition, taking away waste, bringing in oxygen, so cells can metabolize normally again."

BRUCE LIPTON, PHD. Cell Biologist

"Psychologists tell us that 70% of our thoughts are negative and redundant. The new biology, especially epigenetics, reveals how our mind and our perceptions control our genes. The conscious mind, which is the more evolutionary advanced state, is the creative part of our brain.

In contrast, the subconscious mind has some creativity, but it is primarily a habit mind. Nature designed the child's brain for the first six years to download data about the community life and the family and all the principal rules and organizations that are involved. In fact, the child's brain doesn't even express a level of conscious awareness until after six years of age." Since our subconscious mind is a vast storehouse of early learned behavior, it is key to find ways to access this programming, if we wish to change our ways of being that no longer serve us. Many experts find that conventional talk-therapy has inherent limitations.

CANDACE PERT, PHD. Neuroscientist
"The problem with talk therapy is we tend to revisit the hurts and the pains and by constantly going over them, we're digging deeper and deeper grooves. One has to replace that negative conditioning with new positive forms and in fact, substitute new thoughts."

BRUCE LIPTON, PHD, Cell Biologist
"We are learning that talking to the subconscious mind doesn't work. The conscious mind has an identity 'you', but the subconscious mind is more like a tape player. We can talk to a tape player endlessly, but programs will never change in the tape player. The conscious mind learns in different ways from the subconscious mind.

We can go to a psychoanalyst to find out what happened in our past, and the conscious mind will become aware of all the events, yet our life will be exactly the same as it was before we were aware of this information. This is because the subconscious mind does not learn this way and will still have the original programs in it. We are learning that our lives are a print out of the subconscious mind operating 95% of the time.

One of the biggest desires people have is to change their lives. The conscious mind can learn by reading a book, but the subconscious mind requires repeating things over and over again or getting into a brain state by which information can be directly downloaded in the subconscious mind."

HYLA CASS, MD, Integrative Medicine Expert
Dr. Cass is a psychiatrist and leading expert in Integrative Medicine and how emotions, stress, and nutrition affect health. She was inducted into the Orthomolecular Medicine Hall of Fame, and she is the author of more than 10 popular books including, *8 Weeks to Vibrant Health.*

"After many years of medical practice, it's really clear to me that nature is the best healer. Medications have their place, but for almost any kind of condition, we need to understand how we can bring healing to our own body and mind, ourselves. Stress is the key to a lot of illness. We have the daily stresses of life, and then we have the old stresses- the things that are living in our unconscious that we may not even be aware of. When we address those deep old stresses, and clean them up, we are in a much better place to go from 'the stress response' to 'the relax and restore response.' This is what we really need to do to heal ourselves."

CANDICE PERT, PHD. Neuroscientist
"It takes a lot of energy to repress memories and traumas. These bottled up feelings are robbing us of energy that we could use for our healing, our joy, and our creativity. That's why it's critically important to find healthy ways to make other choices.

We now know that there is no separation between the brain and the immune system.

Every emotion plays an important physiological role in our body. Studies of remarkable recoveries have shown that often tumor shrinkage is actually accompanied by a sudden realization that the person is angry with someone. A sudden insight and permission starts to have a profound emotional expression."

BRUCE LIPTON, PHD, Cell Biologist

"We must understand that the nature of our health is not organically based. The new biology based on quantum physics emphasizes energy fields as primary in shaping our material world and our actions, beliefs, attitudes, and emotions all contribute to these energy fields. The new biology teaches us that we need to develop new ways to engage programs in the subconscious mind."

CANDACE PERT, PHD, Neuroscientist

"Energy healing and touch therapy, in a very gentle way, can direct our attention to some very deep old suppressed issues, so that they begin to come out quite dramatically and subtly. You don't even need to go through the trauma that caused the issue. The energy practitioner can enter in a different place, not where talk is initiated, but they can come in through a different area in the psychosomatic network. It's all about the way we're wired up. We have choice unlike other animals. We have choice."

BEVERLY RUBIK, PHD, Biophysicist

"We become what we think. We become the energy field that we create. The energy manifests at the physical level of the body in the blood and the tissues."

Given the proven correlation of our thoughts, feelings and our physical health, the tools that now exist are vital to our health. We live in challenging times. The profoundly exciting aspect is that today we have a range of powerful self-healing practices to improve our health and expand our consciousness. The first step begins with increasing our awareness so that we can chose to learn and grow, heal and open our hearts, and find inner peace. This will help us hear the messages of our own inner guidance. As more of us learn to practice meditation and come into our hearts, we will each know which practices and life-choices suit us best.

CHAPTER 6

THE HEART, MIND, AND SELF-CARE (1)

In addition to investigating energy medicine, scientists, like those cited below, are also looking at the heart and mind in new ways.

Previously, many thought that the brain was the most powerful organ in the body, but studies are now showing that the heart generates the largest electromagnetic signal in the body. In fact, its magnetic field is 5,000 times greater then that produced by the brain. Spiritual traditions have long believed that the heart is the central guidance system for the body and mind.

LYNNE MCTAGGART, Consciousness Expert
"There is some very interesting modern evidence about the heart and brain, that backs up what spiritual masters have been saying for centuries. In modern science we always think that the brain is the main engine of the body and the main antenna for receiving information. But there have been a number of studies demonstrating that actually the heart receives a lot of information earlier then the brain, and even informs the brain."

ROLLIN MCCRATY, PHD., is the author of *The Coherent Heart* and Director of Research, at the Institute of HeartMath, one of the leading organizations devoted to understanding the physiology of stress and heart-brain interactions.

"The heart and brain are uniquely interconnected. 85% of the nerve pathways between the heart and the brain are carrying the signals from the heart to the brain, instead of the other way around. The heart is sending a neural signal first to the brain, and then you see signals in the brain responding. This happens time and again before a future event and then the brain signals the body in a way that we feel conscious of it. The gut is the last to get its heart brain/ body and conscious awareness.

The heart causes a global synchronization signal that synchronizes the body as a whole that sets the tone and the pace for our whole body. When feeling a strong positive or negative emotion, the hormone system activates a cascade of at least 1,400 biochemical changes. A positive emotion is a very different biochemical pattern from a negative emotion, and this is especially reflected in the rhythm patterns of the heart. When we're feeling positive emotions like care, appreciation, love, compassion, the heart beats out a very different message than it does if we're feeling anxious or irritated. We can begin to understand that feeling upset is really depleting us and literally increasing the aging process. It's important to become aware that when we are having feelings of being angry or impatient, we can choose to be more patient and positive. It has profound influences on our short and long-term health and well-being.

These fascinating experiments illustrate the wisdom from the world's great religions and philosophers when they say to 'sing from your heart, put your heart into it.' The heart really is the primary source of the more spiritual aspect and wisdom in our lives. New studies are also showing that both the power of our mind and our intentions dramatically affect our health, our consciousness, and our world at large."

BRUCE LIPTON, PHD, Cell Biologist

"It's now been recognized by conventional science that one-third to two-thirds of all healing, be it drug-related or surgery–related is actually due to something called 'the placebo effect.'"

LYNNE MCTAGGART, Consciousness Expert

"Doctors complain about the placebo effect because they say it messes up drug studies, but the placebo effect is probably the most powerful medicine we have. It demonstrates that as far as our bodies and our brains are concerned, we can't distinguish between a chemical and the thought of a chemical, the thought of a medicine. One of the fascinating aspects about our brain is that it's a little bit dumb. It's this marvel but when it comes to action and thought a brain can't really tell the difference.

One of the most fascinating studies about the placebo effect didn't have to do with the drug at all but an operation. Researchers took a group of patients with arthritis of the knee and gave two-thirds of them an actual operation and one-third a sham operation. Their knees were cut open but they didn't do any operation. What they discovered afterward is that all of the patients, whether or not they got the actual operation, reported moderate improvement. However, the group with the best outcomes was the one with patients who only had the sham operation. This is another example of the power of the mind and the power of thought to heal."

BRUCE LIPTON, PHD, Cell Biologist
"The significance of these kinds of studies is that consciousness through positive thoughts brings about healing in a body, but negative thoughts are equally powerful. They'll work in the opposite direction, and that can actually cause illness and death. The power of thinking, the power of consciousness is equally powerful whether we're thinking positive or negative thoughts."

LYNNE MCTAGGART, Consciousness Expert
"The extraordinary research that's available about the power of intention shows that thoughts affect every aspect of our lives. One argument with a spouse can affect your healing for days. If you have a cut, it will heal a lot slower if you have a negative thought. This suggests that we have to become extremely mindful about what we're thinking and we have to start becoming positive in the way we view the world. We have to realize that what we say and what we think is being heard.

One of the most dangerous things about negative intention is that it's so unconscious. All of us walk down the street having lots of judgments and negative intention, and they have an effect. Also, our media is very negative and that constant seepage of negative intention is having an effect on every one of us. We are all feeling the effect of negative thoughts just as much as positive ones."

BRUCE LIPTON, PHD, Cell Biologist
"The nature of consciousness is very interesting. Our mind really doesn't listen to dialogue but really focuses on images. For example, if I say to myself, 'I don't want cancer', the mind doesn't pay attention to the dialogue 'I don't want' but it does

have an image of a cancer. So it becomes very important to recognize that we have to focus on what we want and not focus on the things that we don't want, because the mind will immediately gravitate to the images of the negative things and actually manifest them.

A way to change these beliefs is to consciously convert our negative thoughts to positive images and visions as a correction factor. The more we repeat this process, the more rapidly the subconscious mind will rewrite the limiting and disempowering programs and create more effective positive visions that we can then manifest."

LYNNE MCTAGGART, Consciousness Expert

"For several decades, a number of scientists in prestigious universities have been engaged in studies showing that thoughts can affect everything from bacteria and algae to animals and plants to complicated things such as human beings. This body of evidence is very robust and it certainly points to the fact that thought is a thing in a sense that affects other things."

CANDACE PERT, PHD, Neuroscientist

"The pendulum is really swinging in mainstream medicine. Not too long ago everything was thought to be genetic. All we heard about was the genetic causes of cancer when in fact the experts agree that less then 2% of all cancers are genetically linked. It's now clear that cancer is a disease of environmental toxicity."

BRUCE LIPTON, PHD, Cell Biologist

"When children are adopted into families with cancer the adopted child will get the cancer with the same propensity as any other natural sibling, yet the adopted child came from completely different genetics. We acquire our personality, which has our beliefs and emotions in it at a very early age in our development, and this affects our whole being.

When we look at the physical body and genes and look at the source of illness, we're really beginning to learn that it's our perceptions and our beliefs and attitudes about life that control not just our behavior, but our biological expression as well, including genes and activity. As more of us begin to understand this, there will be a change in our healing practices toward more personal responsibility in our health and away from feeling like a victim of biology, genes and chemistry."

BEVERLY RUBIK, PHD. Biophysicist

"There's a huge shift going on today in medicine, from the old allopathic biomedical model to a new model that encompasses more of the whole person, body, mind and spirit and is able to deal with our chronic degenerative illnesses today. One of the changes is that enhanced self-care moves to the forefront of the new medicine, that people need to take more self-responsibility for their health and wellness.

We need to understand what's best for ourselves and take those measures really on a daily basis in terms of what we choose to eat, what we choose to do with our time, what thoughts we choose to think, and even thinking positively about our health makes a big difference in the long run."

BRUCE LIPTON, PHD. Cell Biologist
"We now know that genes do not control our traits. It's our perceptions, beliefs and attitudes about life, which in fact control our genes. Rather then blaming everything on the body, we're beginning to see that we are primary in shaping our health and therefore we must be primary in bringing health back to our system."

With the dramatic rise of environmental toxins and a more stressful world, learning dynamic self-healing practices, mind-body methods, and energy techniques has become increasingly important for maintaining optimum health and balance.

BEVERLY RUBIK, PHD, Biophysicist
"I've watched people over the years who practice energy healing and Qigong. All of these energy medicines make substantial changes toward improvement of their health and wellness, their attitude, and improving the health and wellness of those around them.

I see energy medicine changing people one life at a time. This allows them to open toward realizing how powerful their minds really are. They can make the energy shifts in their lives beyond just the flesh, into their personal relationships, into manifesting in the physical world, far beyond the domain of their bodies. This is just the beginning."

CHAPTER 7

ENERGY HEALING

An Introduction to Energy Healing (1)

Energy Healing is an ancient healing method that has been practiced around the world for thousands of years. Energy healing is form of healing where the healer removes blocked energies and then rebalances the flow of energy in the body. Today, there is a resurgence of global interest in energy healing and hundreds of scientific studies are showing positive results.

It's important to note that all energy healing methods are similar, and yet each is unique in its own way. Some of the similarities include:

- The practitioner channels energy from their hands, which can be placed lightly on the body, or slightly above the client's body. The client is fully clothed.
- Energy healing practitioners can treat physical, emotional, and spiritual issues, and the work is useful for chronic and acute conditions.
- The client can be in the same room as the healer or thousands of miles away.
- The clients don't have to believe in energy healing for it to be effective.
- All energy healing sessions have three common aspects: The healer assesses the patient's blocked energies; then

they work to remove the unwanted energy; and then the healer channels restorative energy to rebalance the patient's energy system.

Each healing modality offers its own approach on how to accomplish these aspects, from the very basic to the highly advanced.

Our most recent findings from quantum physics and the biochemistry of emotions have given us new insights as to why and how many energy-healing methods work so deeply and powerfully. Using a wide range of non-verbal, energetic practices, they access alternate pathways to the brain to affect deep healing. As Candace Pert, PhD, explains.

CANDACE PERT, PHD, Neuroscientist
"The energy healing practitioner can come in through a different area in the psychosomatic network and can direct our attention to some very deep old suppressed issues, so that it begins to come out subtly and dramatically."

LYNNE MCTAGGART, Consciousness Expert
"A number of scientists around the world have been looking at studying energy healers to try and isolate what it is they send. They've found that there's an increase in electrical energy, and with it, a surge and voltage. There's also a surge of magnetic energy and there's a huge surge in these bio photon emissions, the current of light coming from the body particularly coming from the healer's dominant hand. We're not talking about ordinary electromagnetic because we know that healing can occur over vast distances. Probably what's going on is much

more complicated. There's probably some sort of quantum effect, which doesn't require any kind of distance that can be the same effect over any kind of distance. Or it may be a combination of all of the above."

BEVERLY RUBIK, PHD., Biophysicist
"Since 1978, I've done numerous studies on energy healing on cell cultures in the laboratory and I've found repeated beneficial effects. Of special note is the positive effect on cells that have been damaged by antibiotics or temperature shocks. When healers place their hands on the cultures or nearby, or even in distant healing cases, the cells recovered faster then the control cultures that were not treated by them. That's a remarkable effect because it shows that the power of energy healing goes beyond the biology of belief or a placebo effect. The fact that cell cultures can respond means that the cells in our bodies are also responding to energy healing, not just our minds, but energy healing is working at all the levels of our being."

LYNNE MCTAGGART, Consciousness Expert
"The perceived wisdom in orthodox medicine is that energy healing has no evidence and does not work. Nothing could be further from the truth. There are at least 150 excellent scientific studies of energy healing and these are those gold standard, randomized double-blind types of studies that are used in science. And they demonstrate a very robust affect."

One of these studies is the study on AIDS, which Lynne discusses in the next section.

LINNIE THOMAS, HTCI, Healing Touch Practitioner, and author of *The Encyclopedia of Energy Medicine.*
"In most of the 200 different modalities I have studied, I find that most healers start with setting an intention for the highest good of the client. A client does not have to believe in what is happening. All he or she has to do is express willingness. The healer is like a garden hose and the energy flows through the healer to the client. I was called into the hospital by one of my clients for his mother. She had had a stroke that morning and was dying. The whole family was there. I had the whole family touch her and then I put one hand on the side of her head and one hand on the other. She had had a serious stroke and the CAT scan showed that 65% of her brain had been damaged. After I began, my hands got very hot and started to shake and I couldn't stop the shaking. The heat got very intense and I was afraid I was going to burn her and all of a sudden, after about 15 minutes of this, she woke up, the paralysis was completely gone, and she was fine. Years later, this woman is still alive and thriving."

BEVERLY RUBIK, PHD. Biophysicist
"The biofield can regulate because it travels at the speed of light, so it totally unifies the organism into a coherent whole and moves the organism into a new dynamic mode. We call that homeodynamics. *I think of the biofield as an orchestra of different energies, different frequencies, just like you literally hear a symphony. These are complex fields of infrared, magnetic energy, visible light, bioelectricity, and probably more.*

And then we may ask, "Who is the conductor?" The mind is. '*Where mind goes, energy flows, and blood and flesh follow'. So the mind is a supreme conductor of this symphony of the biofield and the biofield literally moves at the speed of light because fields do this.* It makes the body a coherent whole in response to thought, and a response to stimuli such as energy medicine. Homeopathy, for example, can work this fast. By contrast to pharmaceutical drugs, which take time to be metabolized and work very slowly, in energy medicine we're actually working at a much deeper levels, and the healing can go much faster.

We're working at a more primary level of life that supersedes the physical because the biofield in my view is the bottom line regulator of the physiology and the chemistry of the body, along with the mind. So if we can work on that level with our medicine, then we can shift ourselves, and self-healing will happen."

LYNNE MCTAGGART, Consciousness Expert
"There was one study looking at magnetic energy emanating from one group of healers and comparing that to the energy emanating from master healers. They found that the master healers essentially generated 1/3 more magnetic energy then the ordinary healer."

In her book, *The Encyclopedia of Energy Medicine,* Linnie Thomas listed energy healing modalities in four categories: Eastern, Western, Spiritual and Shamanic. One Light Healing Touch is listed in the spiritual section, since the teachings are based on Ron Lavin's life experience, his psychic understanding of the true nature of energy, and his esoteric, shamanic, and holistic training.

ONE LIGHT HEALING TOUCH™ with Ron Lavin, MA.

One Light Healing Touch is an international energy healing and mystery school located primarily in the United States and Germany founded by Ron Lavin. The school honors all spiritual traditions and serves the novice and advanced practitioner alike.

Ron Lavin, MA, is a renowned energy healer and gifted psychic who has been featured in the media internationally. He founded the school in 1996, and is also the creator of "One Light Healing Touch Journeys", an audio series of self-healing practices. In 1994, Ron was tested and was found to be running "the master healer energy" frequency. They used a machine measuring magnetic energy and Lavin's healing energy registered about .8 hertz, and they noted "that the strength and quality of that energy was robust."

Gary Schwartz, a world-renowned researcher, did a study of "Masters Healers" and some popular energy healing methods. He found that "Master Healers" averaged about 1/3 more magnetic-field changes-per minute, than the other healers. (3)

Skilled energy healers learn how to access the symphony of energies described by biophysicist, Beverly Rubik, PhD in the documentary, *The Healing Field.* She found that "energy healing frequencies are complex fields of infrared, magnetic energy, bioelectricity, visible light energy, and probably more." Like a garden hose, energy healers allow the energy to flow through them, so they're running this whole symphony of energies described by Beverly Rubik. In OLHT we teach a fundamental '9 Point Protocol' so the healing can be done in a safe, high and ethical manner. We also teach that it's important to 'not be in your mind' during a healing, but be intuitive and open and allow the energy to flow into the client.

RON LAVIN, MA. Founder & Director of One Light Healing Touch™

"Human kind was truly given a profound legacy in hands on healing. Today there is a resurgence of healing all over the world. Energy healing is part of the medicine for an evolving new world. I was born clairvoyant, clairsentient, clairaudient, and claircognizant, which means that I could see, hear, know, and feel the energy of other people and of spirit.

My life has been about receiving these messages and understanding what it is that spirit is guiding me to do. I saw where people were holding energy in their bodies, and would not express what they were feeling or thinking. And I saw that this was a very painful way for people to move through the world.

I've studied with lamas, gurus, shamans and exceptional teachers of all kinds for many years. In the early 1980s, I had a pivotal healing experience. I woke up one morning and had a painful groin and realized after seeing a doctor that I needed a hernia operation. The doctor said that for $5,000 and 4 days of rest I would be fine. I asked him if he knew what was causing the hernia and if he could guarantee me that it wouldn't come back. He said he had no idea what caused it and he was interested in taking care of it but that's as far as he could go.

At the time, I was studying with a gifted Masonic teacher and I asked him about a dream that I had of sewing up this hernia with a silver thread. He said that it would work perfectly, and he would 'hold the energy' for me while I performed this. It took 30 seconds and I was fine one minute after. The dream instructed me to do this again a couple of days later to make sure. So a few days later, I created an etheric silver thread, and sewed it up and I was fine. In that moment I knew and understood to the core of me that my life would be about doing spiritual and energy healing. That was 30 years ago and I've never had a return of the hernia."

RON LAVIN has participated in five remarkable distant healing studies with the National Institutes of Health, including a landmark study on AIDS patients, conducted by Dr. Elizabeth Targ.

"It was an honor to be a part of Dr. Elizabeth Targ's study on end-stage AIDS. I was particularly pleased and delighted when I learned that so many of the participants had a marked decrease in their secondary diseases."

LYNNE MCTAGGART, Consciousness Expert
"The late psychiatrist Dr. Elizabeth Targ conducted one of the most well-researched studies of distance energy healing. She created a study of AIDS patients in the late 1980s before all of the medicine now available to them. They were in the last stages of AIDS. She gathered together an eclectic group of 40 healers around America. None of the healers actually met the people they were going to heal. All they received from Elizabeth was a photo, a T-Cell count and the name of the patient.

Afterwards, she had to conclude that the patients given healings were better in every way. 40% of the patients who were members of the control group who did not get the healing died by the end of the study, whereas all of the patients who had received the healings were not only alive, but also healthier in every regard. They had longer survival, and had fewer side affects and fewer additional illnesses. They were improved in every way."

Ron Lavin has developed a highly experiential teaching program for the One Light Healing Touch School and the students learn a wide-range of self-healing practices and energy healing techniques, to heal themselves and others. In fact, the filmmaker of the documentary and author of this book became a practitioner-instructor after experiencing and seeing many remarkable healings from this work.

Ron Lavin - Clients' Healing Stories (2)

Distant Healing – Spiritual Closure

"I received an emergency phone call on June 1st, 2018 at 9:00 am from a relative saying that her 58-year-old husband had had a heart attack the night before.

She said, 'The paramedics worked on him for more than 30 minutes, including five shocks and four rounds of EPI.' They got only a few pulse beats as the ambulance rushed him to the hospital. He had started breathing with the ventilator and was put into an induced coma. His kidneys were failing. He hadn't regained consciousness, but they were going to try and wake him up the next morning, to see what if any measure of brain damage had occurred, because he had been without oxygen for more than 30 minutes. This was not at all positive. The doctors also said that he had a very low potassium count, but they had no idea why. His heart was at 15% functionality and his blood pressure was low." I asked my relative to send me a picture of her husband and at 9:15 am I began doing a Distant Healing on him. I told my relative, 'I called in The Christ Energy, and have been sending him 'White Light' and calling out to him, in an attempt to assist him in coming back and reentering his body and re-joining his loving family. I sensed that he's experiencing massive confusion and is reaching out and sending all of his love to you and to all of his children'. Roughly 30 minutes later, my relative sent me the following message. 'He just woke up about five minutes ago! He is fighting the vent, but he's calming down a bit. He is alive and awake! For hours he has been asking, 'What happened to me? I don't remember anything. I feel so out of it.' He smiled and said he felt peaceful and grateful to be alive.'

I told my relative that I would do a series of healings on him and see if I could help his kidneys, and in the next couple of weeks, his kidney function began improving. Some months later, the doctors found an inoperable cancerous tumor in his heart and he died quickly by the end of October. My relative and her family said they felt deeply grateful that the distant healings gave them all four extra months, and were a gift which allowed everyone in the family more time to face the situation, and to have closure."

Undiagnosed Long-Held Fear and Past-Life Connections
"My client complained of a lifelong fear and a sense of a foreign presence in her space. I began the session and opened my psychic vision and saw a wolf in her auric field. I began communicating with a wolf that told me that he had been her mascot in a previous life and as they had such a close bond,

he reincarnated with her in this lifetime! I shared this with my client and helped her to connect and communicate with the wolf's energy. I then helped her to release the energy, and afterwards she found a new deep sense of freedom and peace."

Child With Neurological Imbalances

"A mother, who was also a nurse, brought her two-year-old daughter in for a session. She said the neurologist didn't know the cause, but the child had some kind of neurological imbalance. When she walked, she wobbled, and was off-balance. I did a healing on the child as she lay on her mother on the massage table. The next week the mother took her to her neurologist and they were both amazed that when the doctor asked the daughter to walk to the wall chart 10 feet away, she walked easily and with no sense of imbalance."

Diabetes And The Immune System

"I did three distant healings on a client who had a number of issues including, diabetes, low thyroid and anemia. She reported that the healings were very positive and that her recent blood tests showed very much improved results, including a decrease in her blood sugar levels, an increase in thyroid levels, and a general overall wellness that caused her doctor to say, 'You're doing really good!'"

Relief During Cancer Treatments

"My client scheduled a weekly series of energy healing sessions during the six months of her chemotherapy and radiation treatments. She had cancer previously and was nervous about feeling depleted and nauseous during the cancer treatments. Much to her surprise, after each energy session she felt more balanced and energized."

Clients' Experiences During Sessions with Ron Lavin. While these stories are from Ron's clients, they are representative of what clients experience with our practitioners.

"The healing that Ron gave me facilitated a welcome release of long-standing and disempowering patterns. Ron filled me with such an abundance of light and love that my entire being felt enormously joyful and my legs felt like they were sparkling!"

- Julia B (In-person session)

"During the session I saw a vortex of swirling light 'sweep' the body, head to toe, cleaning all muscles and organs! You helped me release fear, doubt, self-criticism, pain, and inflammation, and I forgave others and myself, and released years of negative energies. I felt a sense of Light fill the void. I sensed and felt health, vitality and a deep sense of wellness. A layer of doubt and uncertainly was gone! I bathed in the light and felt a sense of love. Thank you!" - Eduardo R. (Distant Healing)

"I've had gut-wrenching pain for almost two years. I've tried diet, tapping, avoiding allergens, with some little effect. But now after one session, I have had very minimal pain. Thank you!" – Christine B. (Distant Healing)

"During the session, I had a clear sense of total relaxation, almost an ecstatic state. I had multiple visions and I experienced the sensation of your energy passing throughout my body leaving a tingling feeling of well-being." – Dennis W. (Distant Healing)

One Light Healing Touch is based on the philosophy of caring for the whole person. Many of the teachings are derived from Ron Lavin's own spiritual connections and psychic awareness, as is the name of the school itself.

Ron Lavin. MA. Founder & Director of One Light Healing Touch
"By whatever name one calls the divine, there is still only one light of God, "One Light."

We're all born healers. The indwelling god or Light within is the aspect, which heals us, and we may learn to use these same energies to heal others. Healing is any action that increases communication between the Spirit and the body, facilitating one towards greater self-acceptance, integration and wholeness. I feel it's vital to heal the heart, and then to listen to Spirit from the heart, and then to act upon the truths that flow from Source. The heart is the gateway to the soul and must be cleansed and opened to allow for all stages of our spiritual growth." (2)

"Heart healing remains at the core of all of our practices and all of our spiritual work.

Forgiveness is an essential aspect of healing, especially learning to forgive ourselves. As we begin to forgive ourselves we then begin to forgive others and eventually forgiveness becomes a full working partner in our relationship with life. Forgiveness is an essential piece to learn to being at peace with ourselves and to fulfill our purpose for being.

Working with our techniques and practices on a daily basis heals the heart. It releases tension and stress, brings in light, and helps us to come into harmony with our purpose for being." (1)

In addition to the healings students experience during the school, many of our graduates have chosen to become energy healing practitioners, where they work as skilled practitioners.

In our three decades of experience working with thousands of clients, we have found the following patient benefits:

1) Pain relief– This sought-after result is often immediate
2) Increasing the speed of wound and bone healing
3) Improved sense of well-being and quality of life
4) Reduced stress and anxiety
5) Balancing and strengthening the immune system
6) Accelerated recovery from invasive or surgical procedures
7) Increased personal growth and self-awareness
8) Trauma release due to emotional or physical causes
9) Aid in spiritual concerns: end-of-life issues" (2)

One Light Healing Touch™ Instructors - Healing Stories (2)

Infant's Hematoma From Birth Trauma

'I did a One Light Healing Touch session on a mother, shortly after she underwent a difficult and painful home birth. During the session, I worked to help heal her injuries and to release fear and stress from her lower chakras. A week later she brought in her newborn for a session. The difficult birth gave the infant a 3" diameter hematoma on his head, which is a collection of blood outside of a blood vessel. The doctor said it would take about six months for the hematoma to be reabsorbed. In the session, I helped the baby release trauma, pain, fear and stress. The mother, who was witnessing the treatment, said that she could see the hematoma getting smaller and smaller. They visited their pediatrician a month later, and he said he was very surprised that the hematoma was completely gone."- Joachim Deschermaier, Instructor/Practitioner, Germany

Grief From The Loss Of A Child

"My client came for a session desiring clarity about her future goals. I knew from her history that she had experienced the death of a child some years earlier. As I followed the protocols, I scanned her and checked 'the mindful and mindless data,' I psychically saw that she still held a great amount of sadness and pain around her heart and I advised that before looking at the future, we should first work on this issue. 'Mindful data' is something we know about a client, and 'mindless data' is what we tune into with our inner vision. I used our various techniques to release the problematic energy, along with energy of her deceased child and then I filled her with light. After the healing, she felt an immediate upward shift in her energy. A few days later she reported that for the first time in many years, she was able to smile and even feel joy again!" - Penny Lavin, Instructor/Practitioner, New York

Pain From A Car Accident

"I gave a healing to a woman in her 70s, who was seeking relief from the intense pain she had been experiencing along her spine from a car accident some years before. The pain was confined to the sides of her spinal column from the cervical area to the sacrum, and it had not responded well to physical therapy or medication. I was drawn to place my right hand on the center of her chest just below her collarbones and my left hand in the same location under her back. I sent healing energy through her entire skeletal system from this location, until I felt the trauma and misalignment release and harmony return.

After the healing, she reported that the pain was gone, and said that during the healing my hands felt very warm on her body and that everything seemed to melt into my hands. The next day she had no need for the pain medication. Three months later, the pain has not returned." - Julia Ananda, Instructor/ Practitioner, Utah

Intense Pain From Achilles Tendon Injury

"A relative contacted me late one evening, after she suffered a strained Achilles tendon a few hours earlier. Although she was a disbeliever in energy work, she was in intense pain and was desperate for help. She could barely put any pressure on her foot. Before I began, I asked her to focus all of her thoughts into healing her tendon while I was working on her. I followed the OLHT Protocols, and I performed the healing focusing most of my intention on the Achilles tendon area, while connecting with the higher energies of light and spirit. After the healing was complete, she slowly slid off the table and proceeded to stand up. She then walked around the room, and incredulously said, "Oh my God! It doesn't hurt. I can walk on it!" The next day she was able to go to work pain-free. Almost a year later, she has not had any further issues with her Achilles tendon, and has become an enthusiastic supporter of energy healing work." - Jennifer Schnabel, Practitioner, NY

Shoulder Pain And Unexpressed Mourning

"I worked with a client who had resistant shoulder pain, which was continually getting worse. She said it felt like a sword between her ribs. She had tried physiotherapy, but the relief only lasted a few hours. I began a One Light Healing Touch session, by vibrating the 2nd and 4th chakras, and the patient began to connect to a deep sadness in those areas. I then helped her to release the energies, when suddenly the pain in her shoulder flared up.

As I learned in the training, I opened to my inner guidance and I got a visual of 'many strong women, walking through her left side', and sensed that she held ancient ancestral female energies. As the client felt deeper into her feelings, she became immobile, as she sensed the sadness and pain was carried by her female relatives. She was completely surprised by this, as her female relatives had always presented themselves as being very strong! When the client's grandmother was 47, she had lost many female relatives and other family members in an accident. My client began to cry, as she released this deeply held painful old energy. She allowed herself to mourn, and also mourn for her female relatives. My patient saw that in her own life, she too overcompensated, trying to be very strong and to be the best in everything, to cover up the pain. She realized that she had been carrying the pain of others that didn't belong to her, and she learned she could release it, and be loved for being herself! She was astonished that the pain in her shoulder disappeared immediately. I was in awe that this single session was so deeply transformative both physically and emotionally in my client's life!" - Angelica Bingenheimer, Instructor/Practitioner, Germany

Letting Go of Fear of Death

"My mother was diagnosed with metastatic melanoma and I immediately began doing a series of energy healings on her, some in person and some at a distance, following the OLHT Protocols. The cancer initially seemed to retreat with MRI's that showed very little evidence of the disease, but then it returned even stronger. Often when I did healings on her, I felt the presence of her father in spirit. I sensed him lay his hands over mine, assisting with the healing. My mother felt an incredible peace come over her as a result and told me that she no longer feared dying. One night she told me that, after her visitors had left, she smelled the scent of tobacco in her room and we discussed that it seemed that her father was by her side. After she passed, her spirit communicated with me and she thanked me for all of the healing work I had provided her and said she was able to pass peacefully and let go of her fear of death." - Lyn McGuffey, Instructor/Practitioner, Indiana

Intolerable Physical Pain

"My client complained of almost intolerable pain throughout her body for 15 years, which had even forced her to leave her teaching job two years prior. It also caused her to rely on heavy drugs like morphine to cope with her daily chores. When I began the session and scanned her body, I saw a lot of stress and painful energies from physical and emotional injuries. Because of the extent of her issues, I had her attend our OLHT Introductory Workshop, so she could learn the tools for her own self-healing. I also did OLHT healings on her every month, and after a few months she was able to reduce the drugs by 70%, and after two years she was pain-free and able to resume working fully as a primary school teacher." - Joachim Deschermaier, Instructor/Practitioner, Germany

Severe Insect Allergy

"My client has a severe allergy to insect bites and after being bitten by a wasp near her eye, she took her usual medication. However, the next day she contacted me for an energy session and said she was in tremendous pain and that her whole face had swollen up during the night. She said her pain felt like large pressure coming from inside her eye. Her skin was bulging and very bruised. I began the healing by pulling out the problematic energy, and then I worked on cleansing and balancing her chakras, filled her with higher light energy and helped her to ground and relax. At the end of the healing, she looked in the mirror and saw that the swelling was completely gone! Under her eye was a slightly red swollen spot, but her eye was clear. She reported that the 'inside pain' was significantly better." - Angelica Bingenheimer, Instructor/Practitioner, Germany

HEALING TOUCH™

In her book, *The Encyclopedia of Energy Healing*, Linnie Thomas listed Healing Touch (HT) ™ as one of the techniques in 'the Western Category' and it is one of the primary energy healing modalities used by nurses in the U.S. Janet Mentgen, BSN, RN, HNC founded HT™ in 1989, and by adding techniques from many disciplines, Mentgen developed a medically-based energy therapy training program.

LINNIE THOMAS, HTCP, HTCI, MLW, is a Certified Practitioner and Instructor with the HT™ program.
"HT's non-invasive techniques employ the hands to clear, energize, and balance the human and environmental energy fields, thus affecting physical, mental, emotional and spiritual health, placing the client in a position to self-heal. The practitioner accesses the client's body and energy field, and then the practitioner places their hands on or just above the body at specific points to achieve the goal of balancing the chakras and bringing them into harmony with the energy field and physical body. Clients uncomfortable with being touched may request the work be done completely off the body." (2)

Healing Touch™ offers:
* Excellent introductory classes ideal for those who seek a medical and scientific model.

* Techniques that have a scientific basis and practitioners participate in numerous research studies to back up their class materials and theories.
* They have national accreditations, including the American Holistic Nurses Association and are approved for Continuing Education Units for Nurses and Massage Therapists. (2)

Linnie Thomas Clients' Healing Stories

Severe Dental Pain

"I worked on a friend who was in considerable pain following a dental procedure that morning, in spite of having taken some painkillers. I used some HT™ techniques that are designed for reducing pain. The side of my friend's face was quite red from the dental procedure and the rest of her face was pale. During the session, the redness drained from her face. A short while later, my friend jumped out of her chair and began dancing around the room. 'My pain is gone! My pain is gone!' she cried. The pain never returned. (2)

Swelling And Pain From Endometriosis

I was doing a session on my daughter who was in the hospital recovering from a hysterectomy. She was also experiencing severe discomfort due to her endometriosis. They had to move her bowels to work on her hysterectomy, and bowels do not like to be moved and they fuss about it. The third day after her surgery she began throwing up and her bowels stopped working entirely. I began by holding my hands six inches above her body and moving my hands down the body, one at a time with palms facing the body, which is one of the most common ways to soothe and bring balance to the energy system. Shortly thereafter, I saw that it wasn't bringing her relief, so I began using a variation to the technique, which is moving my hands up her body, from her hips, up to her rib cage, towards her heart. I repeated this many times. After about five minutes or so, she breathed a sigh of relief. A few minutes later she fell asleep and slept for sixteen hours. She had no further trouble with nausea." (2)

CHAPTER 8

QIGONG

Qigong is another ancient, powerful self-healing energy practice. It originated in China more than 5,000 years ago. It is a system related to Tai Chi. Now millions worldwide practice the many different methods of Qigong and Tai Chi, that include exercises, breath work, visualizations and meditations, and the latest studies are showing extraordinary results. (Some of the studies are included in this section, and others are in Chapter. 13.)

GARY RENZA is an herbalist and writer, and is a highly respected Qigong Master and Tai Chi Instructor in Cold Spring, New York.

"Qigong is a centuries-old practice whose main purpose is to balance the energy in and around one's body. And at a certain point in their practice one will start to feel this movement of energy. Once they feel the movement of energy, the deep breathing behind the practice of it allows the result to get to a cellular level for healing, for the purpose of longevity. The more we can keep ourselves energetically alive, the more we can keep our bodies alive." (1)

KEN COHEN, from Colorado and California, is a Qigong Master and teaches all aspects of Qigong. He is a renowned China scholar and is the author of *The Way of Qigong* and more than 200 journal articles, and is the winner of the Lifetime Achievement Award in Energy Medicine.

"Qigong to me is very basic, very down to earth. I've been doing this for a little over 40 years, so when I was first starting, I said to my teacher, Master Chan, 'What would you say is the fundamental reason for doing Qigong?' He said: 'We have to master the four virtues of being a human being: 'How to lie down, how to sit, how to stand, and how to walk' But the problem is we are in such a fragmented, such a rushed society, that we're never doing these things in a way that really brings enjoyment. One of the consequences of the quick pace of life of today and the amount of stress that so many people are under, especially racing against the clock, is that the breathing rate tends to be too fast. The average breathing rate for example in the U.S. is about 17 breaths per minute, and if someone is having a problem with anxiety or even a panic attack, it can go up to 22 breaths per minute.

When you practice Qigong within a month of practice, most of my students are breathing at a rate of 7 breaths per minute, which is more the optimal rate. That means that it takes less breaths and less effort to drive the necessary oxygen into your cells. It also means more mental clarity. The brain takes up 2% of the body's weight, but requires 20% of the body's available oxygen. If you can practice a technique that delivers more oxygen to the brain and also slows down the breathing rate so it takes less breaths, less effort to get that oxygen there, there's a dramatic effect on health and energy." (1)

Biophysicist, **BEVERLY RUBIK, PHD.** found dramatic effects in the biofields of Qigong practitioners.

"I measured the biofields of many people who practiced Qigong. In one Qigong class when I measured before and after the class. I found great improvements in their biofields. I found more right and left symmetry, and a smoother, brighter expansion of energy following Qigong." (1)

GARY RENZA, Qigong Master
"Qigong is a wonderful exercise for balancing and healing the mind, the body and the spirit by way of posture, breath and awareness or the regulation of the mind. One student in particular came to me with joint pain and the inability to close her hand. She also had weak bones. After about a year of dedicated practice she came back with the results of her recent test and her arthritis had diminished exceedingly in her hands especially, and her bone density came back stronger." (1)

KEN COHEN, Qigong Grand Master
"We know that at least 75% of all the diseases a person develops as an adult are not due to genetics or what the Chinese would call your original or inherited Chi. Rather we develop these diseases because of behavioral choices that cause either genetic suppression or expression. Even if you've had a family history of three generations of breast cancer, that doesn't mean you're doomed to develop breast cancer. If you make a systemic overall change, then the chances go more in your favor of never developing that illness even if there's the genetic tendency. I've seen so many extraordinary benefits that Qigong has had on cancer and heart disease and diabetes, much of this supported

by very good published research. A group of 48 patients with type II diabetes, adult onset diabetes were all doing Qigong. 95% had normalized blood sugar within one month of regular practice. I've seen similar results among my own students, some of who were on insulin at the start of an 8-week program and at the end of the 8 weeks, with their doctor's permission, they were off of the insulin. So it seems that there is something about Qigong that increases the insulin sensitivity of cells, which is important for all of us if we want to have a healthy metabolism." (1)

Ken Cohen has demonstrated the powerful nature of Qigong in many hospital studies across the country. One study found that Ken's brain waves changed more than 70% while practicing Qigong, including strong gamma waves, which are linked with the prevention of dementia. Ken also practices Medical Qigong, also called Chi Healing, which is showing exceptional results both in China and the U.S.

KEN COHEN

"It's called external Chi healing. Essentially, the healer uses the energy field from his or her hands to affect a new state of balance in the client. Qigong has a very bright future. It's growing really quickly. More and more doctors are making referrals to Qigong and Tai Chi practitioners for both patient education and for themselves, to heal and prevent burnout. If you're dealing with patients all day long it's easy to get burned out. So we need Qigong also for the healer to take care of him or herself." *(1)*

BEVERLY RUBIK, PHD. has found that ideally, all energy practitioners need to take the time to practice, to achieve the most beneficial results.

"My research has shown that it takes many classes to produce a lasting change in the bio field - whether it's yoga, Qigong or visiting an energy healer, doing meditative practices. All of these can produce profound changes in the biofield, but they need to be regular practices. I found a threshold of about two years of a regular practice to make a lasting change in the energy field." (1)

Qigong – An Overview (2)

The ancients called our energy, Qi. Qigong means "Qi Energy Training". The detailed knowledge of the Qi (energy) and its flow of Yin and Yang in the body and in the various organs became the basis of traditional Chinese medicine. They learned to use a range of tools, including herbs, foods, acupuncture, and movement to clear blockages. They found that our well-being, and even our very existence depend on how free flowing and strong this force is in our body. The ancients discovered that by practicing Qigong, one could achieve improved health and longevity.

GARY RENZA, Qigong Master and Tai Chi Instructor
"Energy is everywhere. The entire universe exists because of energy. Gravity and inertia are forces of nature, which impact our very existence. Humans are essentially light energy, and we give off heat, and produce electric and magnetic currents.

The Taoists categorized it as 'universal Qi, earth Qi and human Qi'. Therefore, we have a need to understand the energy inside of us as well as the energies constantly affecting us outward. Our internal Qi flows inside of our bodies through a matrix of pathways called meridians that nourish every cell and support all of life. We also emit external Qi, which protects us like body armor from external forces, i.e. disease, pathogens, pernicious influences and strikes and blows to the body during martial combat.

Qigong means, 'energy – work'. Qi is energy and Gong is the time and effort it takes to achieve a purpose or goal. Qigong is an energy practice, whereby over time the practitioner learns to first sense the Qi, then one learns to cultivate, circulate, and condense it."

KEN COHEN, Qigong and Tai Chi Grandmaster
"One of the greatest Qigong masters of all time, Wang Xiangzhai (1885-1963), was fond of saying, 'The ordinary is the extraordinary'. We discover mystery and beauty in the everyday: how to sit, how to stand, how to move, even how to breathe with appreciation, awareness, and grace. Qigong is neither esoteric nor exotic. The only 'secrets' to be learned are mastered through dedicated practice."

JACK LIM is an acclaimed Qigong Grand Master. He was born in Australia and was sent back to China by his parents at the age of 14 to study Chinese culture. There he also met and studied with great Qi Masters for 30 years. Jack later returned to Australia where he has become renowned worldwide for teaching The Great Stork Qigong and Qi Healing.

He also spreads healing music throughout the world through his Qi Energy music. Jack Lim believes that he has been fulfilling his destiny, becoming a bridge between East and West.

A number of years ago, I was fortunate to attend a workshop with Jack in Los Angeles where he taught the exquisite Qigong Healing Walk. I found it deeply powerful and I still practice it regularly. It brought me a profound sense of balance, peace and connectedness. He is a gift to all who know him!

Many years ago Jack began introducing Qigong in America at holistic health exhibitions, where he did a convincing demonstration to help conference participants understand the importance of Qi and its flow, since it was something they could not see or feel.

"I would ask for a volunteer to stand in front of me several yards away, with their back towards me. I would push my hand forward without touching and the crowd would be amazed to see the volunteer sway and bend forward. After the volunteer straightened up I would pull my hand back and this time there was a sudden sway towards me. I would then explain what the ancients in China had discovered thousands of years ago; that was the Life force that I had just demonstrated. They found that our well-being, or even our very existence depended on how free-flowing and strong force was in our body. Extreme emotions and stress are often the basic cause of many ailments. The practice of Qigong movement works the best when the student develops a regular practice. I believe every person is born with the power of the Qi and I've seen that Qigong develops the potential of each individual. I developed a particular form called The Great Stork Qigong, which has helped people worldwide for many years."

Qigong Healing Stories (2)

There are now thousands of Qigong lineages that have developed over the centuries. Traditionally, knowledge about Qigong was passed from an adept master to students in elite unbroken lineages. They encompass body-movement practices, meditations, sound work. Some Qigong Masters practice "External Qi Healing, also called Medical Qigong" where they give powerful Qigong Energy sessions to clients. The inspiring stories below are from students who have studied with a variety of Qigong masters.

Ken Cohen's students' healing stories

Diabetes - "I was diagnosed with diabetes about six and a half years ago and my blood sugar was 79 ½. I was on medication for probably a year and I went to the doctor and I asked him how long I would have to be on medication, and he said 'For the rest of your life!' I knew I had to try to improve my health, so I began working with Ken and did my Qigong practice daily. After a while, I threw my pills away and kept monitoring my blood sugar. I went to my doctor and showed him the numbers and he said 'You're right, you don't need them any more!' So doing Qigong has been good for me and has brought me much better health." – Bob C. (1)

Chronic Fatigue – "When I came to study with Ken I was exhausted, emotionally exhausted, physically exhausted and to the extent that I would call it chronic fatigue, was also depressed emotionally. From the day I started working with the primordial Qigong it was like taping into a nurturing force that was everywhere. My energy levels started to return. My relationships with people became better, more harmonious and I was naturally happy to see my friends." - Paul R. (1)

Jack Lim's Great Stork Qigong Is Useful for Many Conditions

Balancing the Whole Body

"I have been teaching Jack Lim's The Great Stork Qigong in Fyresdal, Norway for many years and it works remarkably well for a host of problems. It's really a system for balancing the whole body. It has helped people with migraine headaches, digestive disorders, insomnia, different kinds of pain, depression, infertility, to those coping with stress and more." - Erik Skjervagen, Qigong Master, Norway

Migraine headaches

"I had a client who was a Western medical doctor, and who suffered from serious migraine headaches for many years. She tried every possible Western treatment, but the headaches continued to get worse, to the point where she could barely work. She relied exclusively on Western medicine for pain relief. I had offered her acupuncture but she refused. In desperation she came for an appointment and we started with acupuncture. She felt only limited improvement, so I offered to teach her Qigong.

After three months of practicing The Great Stork Qigong her attacks lessened considerably, and after three more months, they disappeared completely! She then felt so good that she stopped her Qigong practice, but when the migraine attacks returned, she resumed her Qigong practice and has not had another migraine and has had no other treatment. "- Erik Skjervagen

Compromised Immune System

"When I was 15 years old, I contracted Glandular fever. Being unaware of this, I went to hockey practice and took a blow to my abdomen, which ruptured my spleen due to its being swollen from the Glandular fever. My spleen had to be removed by emergency surgery that same night, and my medical personnel said that my immune system would be so severely compromised and that I would need to take antibiotics for the rest of my life to prevent infectious diseases. Since that was not an option for me, I sought out complementary therapies and studied Qigong with Grand Master Jack Lim in Melbourne, learning movement, breathing, and meditations.

As a student and now teacher of Qigong for over 25 years, I have been pleased to experience significant improvement in my immune system and general well-being. I am physically fit and active, and working as a Student Counselor at a secondary school. I do not take any medications and rarely need to see a doctor, other than routine check-ups. Five years ago, I started teaching the *Qigong Anti-Cancer Walk* to people with cancer in the local community This group has been an incredible success, with most of the original participants still attending and benefiting from this therapeutic activity and meditation." - Glenda Channells, Qigong Master, Australia

Pain and Emotional Release

"I practice and teach Jack Lim's The Great Stock Qigong, and have seen great improvement in people with joint and back pain, depression and anxiety. I have seen students cry without warning, and smile and laugh. One feels there is great emotional release in doing the work. Students gradually surrender to the flow of the gentle nurturing field, so soft, yet full of strength, flowing around the body and through the body. Students enter and allow the Qi to guide them in the surrender to the Qi, and the magic works! I feel if one can be patient, and maintain a regular practice, 'The Stork' will provide many wonders." -Anthony Barker, Qigong Master, Australia

Healing Stories Using A Range of Qigong Methods

Qigong to Support Cancer Therapy

"I was diagnosed on February 5, 2018 with an aggressive malignant tumor behind my right eye, which also created a detached retina. A few weeks later I had radiation at Columbia University Presbyterian Hospital in New York, with surgeon, Dr. Brian Marr. I was fortunate to have been guided to Dr. Marr, because he was especially open to my incorporating my Qigong healing work into my treatment. I've been a practicing Qigong teacher and healer for many years, and I used all the Qigong tools available to me, including Medical Qigong treatments, Chinese diet, Chinese herbal prescriptions and Acupuncture and Qigong Intensive Healing at KoKolulu Farm, Hawaii.

On July 10, 2018, we were all gratified to learn that the tumor was diagnosed as being gone, by my Columbia University Presbyterian Hospital doctors! Dr. Marr said that he had never seen a tumor dissolve so quickly in his 20 years of experience, and has never seen an eye heal as well as mine did, post-surgically. In addition, as of November 2018 my vision has continued to improve, but is still limited. The location of the tumor normally would have a prognosis of non-correctable vision loss - in one to five years! Because of my personal experience, in the future, I plan to use my Qigong training and work with cancer survivors and those who are chronically ill." -Richard Clegg, Qigong Teacher/Qigong Therapist, New York

***Gary Renza's Student*: Balance, Concentration and Joint Pain**
"My student Aaron is a dedicated Qigong practitioner. He loves the outdoors and being physically active. When he started Qigong, his balance was poor, he had trouble concentrating, eye-hand coordination was a challenge and he had joint pain in his knees. He practiced Qigong daily with a routine tailored to his specific needs.

With a positive attitude and dedicated correct practice (body, mind and breath awareness), Aaron has substantially improved his balance and coordination. The slow mindful movements helped lubricate his joints and improve his concentration and focus. When I asked him about his joint pain he replied, 'what joint pain?"

***Gary Renza's Student*: Diabetes And Weight Loss**
"My student Dan is a professional, with lots of stress in his work environment. Dan was overweight with poor eating habits and eventually developed adult diabetes and had to give himself insulin shots twice a day. He started Tai Chi to help minimize his stress levels and perhaps lose some of the weight.

Over time, he enjoyed Tai Chi so much that he included Qigong as part of his daily routine. He lost the weight with the help of proper diet, his ability to cope with his stress levels greatly improved and his concentration at work and at home was noticeably better.

But what surprised Dan the most is that his diabetes had so improved that he no longer needed insulin shots and was able to take pills instead! Dan now teaches Tai Chi and no longer needs any medication to control his diabetes. He is able to maintain his blood sugar through diet, exercise and a daily routine of Tai Chi /Qigong."

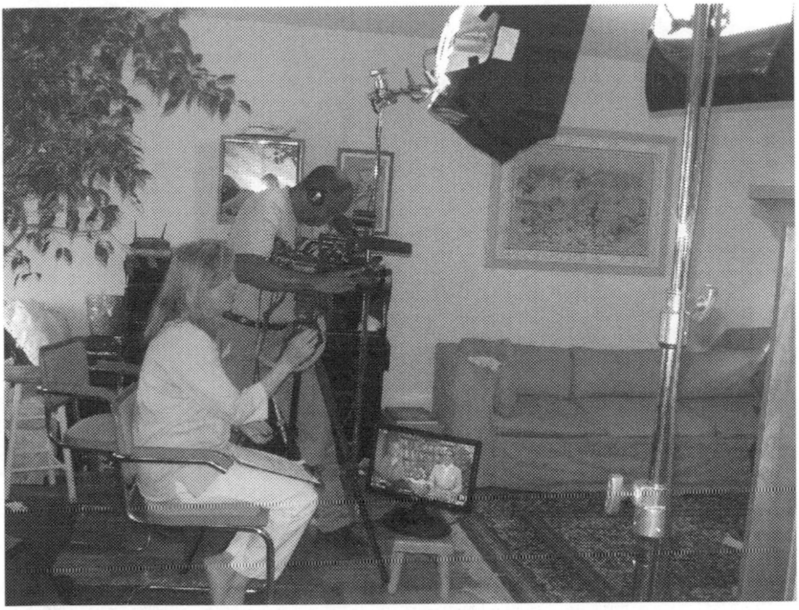

Author and Filmmaker Penny Lavin interviewing for the documentary.

Bruce Lipton, PhD., Cellular Biologist and Author

Lynne McTaggart, Consciousness Expert and author

Beverly Rubik, PhD., Biophysicist

Candace Pert, PhD., Neuroscientist and Author

Hyla Cass, MD., Integrative Physician and Author

Ron Lavin, MA, founder of One Light Healing Touch
Photo by Tom French

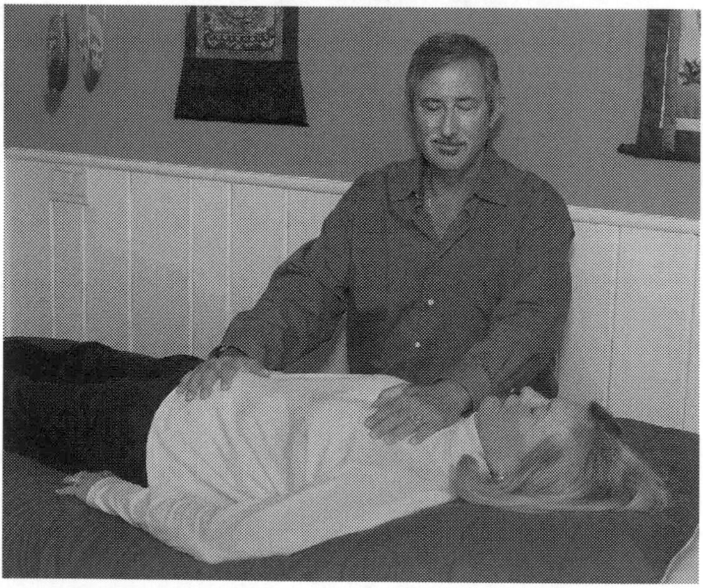

Ron Lavin, MA, giving an energy healing.
Photo by Tom French

Ron and Penny Lavin
Photo by Tom French

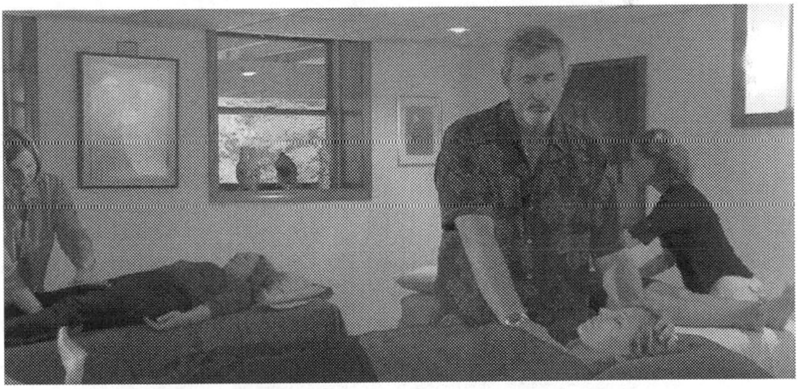

Ron Lavin, MA and One Light Healing Touch students

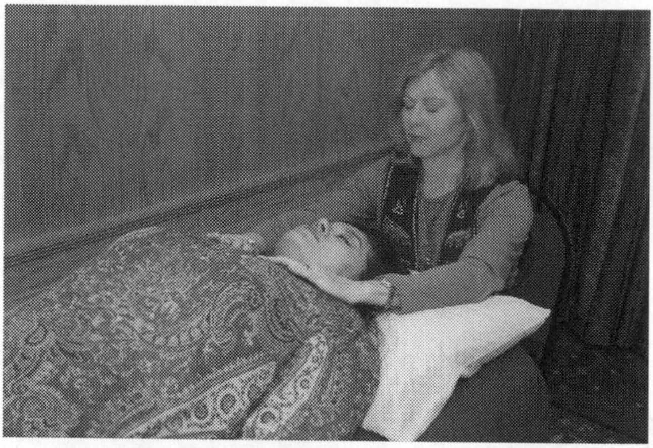

Penny Lavin giving an energy healing
Photo by Tom French

Linnie Thomas, HTCP
Photo by Jaya Thompson

Ken Cohen, Qigong Grandmaster- A posture from Coiling Silk Qigong
Photo by Doug Ellis Photography

Jack Lim, Qigong Grandmaster
Photo courtesy of Jack Lim

Gary Renza, Qigong Master - Tiger posture from the 5 Animal Frolics Qigong set

Jerry Epstein, MD., Mental Imagery Expert

CHAPTER 9

MENTAL IMAGERY (1)

Mental Imagery is another ancient and powerful healing method that has come to the forefront in modern health care. As we look beyond the limitations of conventional therapy, experts are searching for new ways to affect consciousness and deep healing. Mental imagery is proving itself to be a remarkable doorway into the human psyche.

BRUCE LIPTON, PHD, Cell Biologist
"The mind is only 5% of our consciousness, and while that is perfect for receiving informational talk, affirmations, and for reading inspirational books, in order to really heal and change ourselves, we need to find new ways to get into the 95% of our sub-consciousness and unconsciousness if we really want to change our behavior." (1)

One striking mind-body modality is mental imagery. It allows images to work directly on our subconscious minds. Mental imagery incorporates Western spiritual therapeutics, emphasizing the use of imagination and will.

THE LATE JERRY EPSTEIN, MD. of New York City, also known as Dr. Jerry, was a psychiatrist and a leading pioneer in mental imagery and integrative medicine. He was the director of the American Institute for Mental Imagery, which is now being lead by his wife and long time collaborator, Rachel Epstein, L.Ac. (Licensed Acupuncturist) The Institute offers classes and private sessions. Dr. Epstein has authored many CD sets, and seven books including the bestseller, *Healing Visualizations and We Are Not Meant to Die,* which he co-authored with his wife.

"I was a traditional psychiatrist and psychoanalyst, and I came to this mental imagery work in 1974 when I visited Israel. By great good fortune, I was introduced to a woman named Collette Aboulker-Muscat who seemed to be getting and achieving greater results in the work she was doing than I had through my conventional practice. I had never heard of mental imagery, but I became her student for nine years. I learned that it is really the application of Western spiritual life into a therapeutic framework. The range of the usage of mental imagery is unlimited. It's used for so many different kinds of circumstances and conditions, physical, emotional, social, mental, moral, that it is applicable to any kind of circumstance you can think of.

Mental imagery has a long and distinguished history. It goes back to ancient Egypt and the ancient Near East, and in fact we call it the hieroglyph of the mind. As such, it is the natural and true language of inner life. We, in turn, use it as a way to direct our being to change and to heal, and to shift our direction in life. The body responds to images. It responds to this inner language.

We generally tend to do it quickly, because we it is a homeopathy of the mind. It's a micro input for a macro output. It only takes a few seconds to up to 30 seconds. You do it when you wake up in the morning to start your day. You do it at night at the end of the day. The way to do the imagery practice is for 21 days. We know that it takes up to three weeks to change a habit or break a habit. It is something that anyone can do. Mental imagery allows us to get beyond our typical emergency, stressful reaction.

When an emergency takes place or what we consider to be an emergency, we act in a natural physiological way, which is called fight or flight. That happens no matter whether the emergency is a real emergency or not. If somebody has a gun to your head and is about to pull the trigger or it's a false emergency which most everything is, which is some kind of projection into the future that something dangerous is about to happen, that's going to be a threat to my life in some way, shape, or form, our reaction is the same.

Whatever it is, the emergency state stimulates the outpouring of a lot of chemicals and hormones, and processes in the system to gear up for the emergency. There's no true outlet for it to take place. You're sitting in the middle of your living room waiting for that phone call because you're expecting some kind of answer to something and it doesn't come. That is 'the emergency' and the body responds and begins pouring out these chemicals to gear you up, but there's no place for them to go. There's no true outlet, so they start to break down in the system and they become poisons. Continuously doing this to ourselves as we do chronically, these systems wear out and they become aged, and they start to get old. As they get old, the decay sets into our bodies and the medical profession comes in and defines that as disease.

It's not a disease. It's a matter of decay. It's something that we can reverse and that's where the mental imagery comes in because mental imagery is a process to reverse the decay. It sets you off on a new course of life in which you are able through the imagery process to optimize your healing process and to stop the emergency states."

Dr. Jerry's Students Share Their Thoughts on the Value of Mental Imagery

"Basically I would say mental imagery is like having a treasure chest. You can just reach in there and pull out anything you need, and it's all inside of you." - Beth D.

"Mental imagery has allowed me to learn to live in the present moment and not be defined by my past history. I work as an artist and I've also felt that when I come into the studio now, I have a blank canvas and I don't bring a lot of baggage with me. I'm able to go into myself and find the beautiful things there that I can learn to express." - Denise S.

"I was deeply unhappy and felt that life just wasn't going the way I wanted it to. Mental imagery has given me a way and a direction away from that life. I have a lot of fun now and I basically feel like I dance through life." – John H.

Jerry Epstein's Healing Imagery literally saved the life of patient Greg Moore.

GREG MOORE, Mental Imagery Student

"Just over a year ago I had a massive heart attack and it turns out that I actually needed a new heart. I went on the waiting list to get a heart transplant, which ended up taking ten months before I found a suitable donor. The heart surgery itself was a major success except three days later there was a major complication with my leg of all things. The leg rejected the transplant. When I awoke from anesthesia, the doctors were telling me that it looked like the only option was going to be amputation, which was certainly alarming to me.

I said we need to look at other options because I'm not ready to go that route. Over that weekend, one of Jerry Epstein's practitioners came to visit me and taught me a few exercises of imagery, and I applied them.

When I woke the next morning, I was beginning to move my toes slightly and found sensation in my foot that previously had no sensation or movement. I continued the exercises and within a few more days after that, I was walking, much to the surprise and delight of my nurses and doctors."

GERALD EPSTEIN, MD. Mental Imagery Expert
"The exercise that I'd given you is one of the exercises that we do for nervous system regeneration. You've actually regenerated your nervous system, and it was shown by the studies they did on your nerves because they took electrical studies of your nerves in your muscles while you were going through this process, and where it was dead to begin with, they saw that it came back to life. That's what gave the doctors the awesome feeling that they've never seen anything like this."

GREG MOORE, Mental Imagery Student
"When I go back to the hospital now, the nurses and doctors are rather amazed to see me walking in without any assistance. I feel like I can enjoy life again and just get back to normal. I'm a big band leader and I feel like I can finally get back to living

again, and certainly through-Jerry Epstein's Mental Imagery, I can do just that, start living again."

ALAN GASS, MD. is the head of the heart transplant team that worked on Greg Moore. He is the Medical Director of Cardiac Transplantation and Mechanical Circulatory Support at Westchester Medical Center.

ALAN GASS MD, Westchester Medical Center

"After several days of using imagery, Greg was scheduled to go to the operation probably to have his leg amputated. When the vascular surgeon opened up the incision, he was amazed at not only the degree of lack of progression, but he actually saw the muscle becoming pinker and looked like it was healing. It was not anything that we had done. It was really, I think, what the imagery had done.

The reason I have so much confidence in mental imagery is because of a personal experience I had two years ago. I was riding my bike in Central Park and had an accident with another rider, and fell, and broke my hip. When I went to the emergency room, they did an x-ray. What I had was a crush fracture of the hip, but also the neck of the hip was fractured and there was a gap in the bone. It was about a millimeter close to requiring surgery, but we opted to do physical therapy to avoid surgery, and then I adopted mental imagery.

My imagery exercise was using a visual like a baker's tool that is used to squeeze out icing on a cake. I envisioned that I was using liquid bone and I was putting it into that gap in the bone. Within a few weeks, my second x-ray showed this fluffy material inside that gap and the orthopedic surgeon was amazed, and he said, 'That looks like bone.' I was not surprised and within two months I was back on my bike. I avoided surgery and I was back on my bike riding 50 miles within two months after a hip fracture."

It's important to note the difference between visualizations and mental imagery. Many athletes today actively practice visualizations, where they see the action needed and they repeat the process endless times in their mind, but mental imagery is a creative and spontaneous action. Mental Imagery invites you to be in the present moment, while visualizations follow a routine of already known images.

GERALD EPSTEIN, MD, Mental Imagery Expert
"The difference between mental imagery and visualization as I see it, is that visualization is something that you conjure up, a goal that you intend about something known to you, and you have a certain result in mind such as athletes who use it all the time. It's used in baseball, golf, and skiing. You can visualize the whole course as you're going down hill, so you get yourself into an experience where you're getting to an outcome that you are intending to manifest. On the other hand, in Mental Imagery, the image itself is a spontaneous act of discovery where you don't know what you are going to come up with, and it then gives you an insight, an understanding about your life, something unexpected and spontaneous. Everyone has the ability to use the power of mental imagery. The power lies within you to do that. You don't need to depend on something outside of yourself."

An Overview Of Mental Imagery (2)

As with many healing modalities, which originated within the ancient model, like energy healing, Qigong, and sound healing, in mental imagery, the practitioner looks at disease in a completely different way from the current conventional model.

Gerald Epstein, MD, Mental Imagery Expert
"The conventional model of health care and the ancient model look at disease in entirely different ways. The ancient system of health care always put the sufferer directly into the position of being responsible for his own or her own condition. The tools were given to the person to take part actively in finding their own way to their own healing." (2)

Over the years, I have been delighted to become friends with Jerry and Rachel Epstein. I also worked with Jerry and learned about the amazing toolbox of mental imagery. Mental Imagery is a remarkable and ancient process of creating a potent image and having it seed our consciousness and unconscious. The protocol is to do it first thing in the morning, and again at dusk, and then just before you go to bed. The client should do the imagery for 21 days, then stop for a week, and begin again if it is needed. It's best to do it sitting up, so the spine is straight, and you don't fall asleep. You begin with a long exhale, with a 'soft jaw,' followed by three short inhales and two more long exhales.

This breathing technique connects us with our parasympathetic nervous system, which allows the imagery to penetrate more deeply into our unconscious. I found mental imagery to be extraordinarily helpful on a wide range of issues for both chronic and acute conditions. Many of our One Light Healing

Touch clients have experienced the profound benefits of this simple and amazing protocol.

Gerald ("Dr. Jerry") and Rachel Epstein, L.Ac., Mental Imagery Experts
"Mental Imagery is a powerful tool for healing physical and emotional disturbances, mending relationships with others, and tapping into our deep source of wisdom and creativity. Almost anyone can learn how to apply this simple tool to reverse chronic daily disturbances and attitudes or to find solutions to seemingly impassable roadblocks in their lives. And, it takes only a few seconds to a minute to do.

The word *healing* in the English language also means whole, heal, and holy, so holy, health and healing are all connected to each other. Almost invariably, whenever there's a physical malady, there's a social disturbance. The ancient Hebraic model teaches that the fabric of our life existence is a social, moral matrix. And when there's a rip in the fabric, when the mantle is torn apart, what comes out of it are physical, emotional, and mental disturbances as signs of a problem in the social moral matrix of our life.

In the mental imagery healing process, we work with the whole expression of the self. The self is expressed through the five facets of existence; physical, emotional, mental, social and moral. It is an integrative system, in which they are all reflecting each other. For example, if a client says 'I have heart trouble', the question we would ask, without neglecting the physical, would be 'Have you been experiencing heart ache recently?" 'Have you lost a love relationship?' There is a healing function when you help the client connect to the cause of the issue. They take an active part in their own healing, because these other areas can be talked about, felt, and can be corrected.

This process is a mutual participation with the client and mental imagery practitioner. In the traditional medical model, almost everything that happens to us is called disease, which is a false emergency, flight or fight mode. Continually doing this to ourselves wears out our systems, but mental imagery is a process to reverse the decay, and gives your unconsciousness ways to reverse the toxicity and create anew. Imagery is an example of the homeopathic principle of a micro input for a macro output, where we become the agents of our own change.

When we engage in mental imagery, we turn away from the ordinary material reality, for a moment, to tune into another reality where we discover a new belief – a new possibility for living that we can bring back to our everyday reality. How does this work? The image gives form to a belief. It gives us a greater concrete awareness of what is otherwise experienced as something more abstract. What we conceive in our "belief-incubator," we can perceive as an image, and then birth it in our everyday reality. We can co-create our world. We have been given free will and choice. Our creations can be life extending or life ending. In short, imagery is a powerful way to actively manifest our beliefs."

Dr. Jerry's Mental Imagery Healing Stories (2)

The Social Matrix of Illness: Healing from Hepatitis C and Autoimmune Disorder

"My client is a wife and mother of three young children, who came to me suffering from Hepatitis C, an autoimmune disease of the liver. Her doctor told her that she was going to die, having only months to live, as there was no known cure for this. When she came to see me, we broadened the picture of her life, beyond her mere physical condition. She was having a difficult time with her mother-in-law who had created a great deal of divisiveness in the marriage, telling her son to leave her.

Together we worked on two fronts: correcting her relational difficulties as well as using mental imagery to heal her liver. I instructed her to imagine the surface of the liver as a mirror and see any areas with spots that needed to be cleaned. She was to take a very soft golden brush and clean away any dark spots she saw. Then she was to go to the underside of the liver, and see the spots there, clean that, and do that three times a day for 21 days. Meanwhile, she took charge of her marriage, telling her husband that their marriage could not continue in the shadow of his relationship to his mother, and that his mother was no longer welcome in the house. Speaking up and reversing her habitual habit of being 'enslaved' to her husband, she took charge of her distressing emotional states, the anxiety and fear. After six months, her liver enzymes were normal and a biopsy showed no abnormal cells. She has been healthy ever since.

Regeneration of the Optic Nerve

My client, a man who was quite successful in his worldly life, came to see me because of serious eye problems. He had atrophy of the left optic nerve and lens deformation of the right eye. His physician had told him that his condition was incurable. He was attuned to the spiritual aspect of life, however, and had some inkling that his blindness was connected to some error in his spiritual life. He came to me seeking mental imagery work.

As is customary in the practice of spiritual medicine, I asked him about the circumstances surrounding his vision loss. What was he not seeing? What did he not want to look at? Was he suffering any guilt feeling? (Remember that Oedipus, the legendary Greek king, blinded himself out of guilt for committing a moral error.) He was decidedly intent on healing himself and was eager to uncover intimate and sometimes morally unpleasant details of his life. These details became important elements in the successful treatment. Our educative-therapeutic work consisted of making corrections for his moral indiscretions, along with practicing specific imagery exercises to restore his vision. The imagery exercises had him clean out his eyes, take in air through his pupils to move the aqueous fluid properly, and cleanse his lenses; a sanctified being (in his case, Jesus Christ) would spit in his eyes to enhance healing.

My client physically bathed his eyes in healing water that he obtained from a religious healing center in North America (analogous to Lourdes in France). He made restitution to all those whom he had wronged, wherever he could. This restitution was usually in monetary form, forgiving the debts of those who owed him and maintaining a generous attitude in the face of all this forfeiture. My client is a naturally generous man, and he was financially able to carry out these actions. He was able to make the corrections rather easily and without resentment since he knew he was making them for his own self-healing. He received back an unanticipated outpouring of love from those to whom he made restitution, including two ex-wives and a relative whose $75,000 debt he forgave. At the end of six months, his vision began to improve. At the end of a year his vision was restored so that he could work normally and he was able to drive his car again.

Creating New Beliefs: Healing from Herpes

My client was a young woman who suffered from herpes genitalia. She had numerous outbreaks, took medication, and was told incorrectly by the gynecologist that her condition was 'incurable.' She was understandably unhappy about this curve ball in her life that has so many unpleasant social implications. We embarked on a program of imagery practice, which she took to readily.

After a period of three weeks of faithfully practicing her healing imagery exercise three times daily, I recommended she go for a blood test to see if the condition had cleared up. Her previous test revealed the presence of herpes genitalia. The new test showed the absence of genital herpes. Here is a summary of the physician's report verifying this finding.

'Good news — all the recent lab tests that you did were negative. No signs of any STD's and you do have immunity to shingles. All STD-tests negative. The HIV, hepatitis b or hepatitis c tests were negative also!'

Healing from Allergies

My client, a young man, appears complaining of multiple allergic sensitivities, particularly chemical substances in the environment. The sensitivities began with a respiratory difficulty experienced when living in an apartment laden with mold. He finally moved to a new location some distance away. It was there he developed the chemical and other allergies. I asked him for the opposite of chemical sensitivities. He responded 'clean air.' I asked for the image of 'clean air.' He immediately said, 'I'm at a beach taking in the pure air there.'I suggested that he say to himself 'cleansing,' feel it, and have a physical sensation. This was the homework I assigned him:

each time he felt distressed by a sensitivity response to an environmental danger to shift to the image of seeing himself at the beach breathing in the clean salt air. He was to say to himself 'cleansing,' feel it, and have a physical sensation. This experience may take only a few seconds and is using Imagery within the homeopathic principles. He reported that he was feeling lighter, breathing easier, and sensed his chest opening.

Healing from Hepatitis C

My client was suffering from Hepatitis C. She told me that she liked working as a commercial artist but really loved to paint. I told her to paint a perfectly healthy liver, and hang it next to her bed and stare at it every morning when she wakes and again when she goes to sleep, and said, imagine that your liver is as perfect as that painting. She was skeptical and expressed doubts and confessed her fears of slowly dying with chronic pain from cirrhosis. I shared that-40% of people with chronic Hepatitis C live out their entire life with no symptoms and die of old age. Just be in that 40%. I lent her an illustrated medical encyclopedia and told her to study the healthy liver as she rendered it with acrylic paint on watercolor paper. She said it took two hours and looked perfect. She bought a frame, hung it on her bedroom wall, and focused on it as if it were an exact replication of her own liver.

I told her to get annual blood tests to keep an eye on her liver enzymes, eat healthy and stay away from toxins—drugs, alcohol, cigarettes and processed foods. That was twenty-five years ago, and she is now fifty. Her liver enzymes are as low as they were when she was first diagnosed. They are only slightly elevated, just enough to show that the virus is still in her system but it is dormant. She recently just got a liver ultrasound that showed her organ is the perfect size and color. Just like the one in her painting.

Creating An 'Opposite Image.' The following three imagery practices are one-minute each and done by creating an opposite kind of image to facilitate healing.

Bursitis: A middle-aged man complained of bursitis, inflammation of the bursa in his shoulder, which had been bothering him for months. It started when someone he deeply loved and respected betrayed him. He realized, on reflection, that he wanted to "smash" 'smash' or punch the betrayer violently. The bursitis reflected his resistance of committing such an act. He could hardly lift it away from his side. Taking aspirin was his only relief.

When I asked him to tell me the opposite of bursitis, he said 'rejuvenation'. I asked, "What 'What image is connected to rejuvenation?' Closing his eyes, he replied, 'A field of lilies. Very beautiful.' I said 'Feel that rejuvenation and get a physical sensation, if one comes.' A faint smile crossed his lips. I told him to say, 'Bursitis be gone!' and to see it skipping away, disappearing into the horizon. Then say 'thank you' and breathe out and open your eyes.' He opened his eyes and was able to lift it away from his side without pain. I told him to repeat the process whenever he was aware of experiencing the difficulty until it was resolved to his satisfaction.

Sciatic Pain: A young woman in her mid-30s was experiencing sciatic pain running down her left leg. I asked her who the 'pain in the ass' was that she wanted to kick. She absorbed the shocking question for a moment and replied her brother, whom she was in conflict with at the time. She responded to the reverse of pain as 'no pain.' With eyes closed, she saw emptiness, felt immediate relief of pain, said "Pain be gone," and saw pain skipping away from her and disappearing. Saying 'Thank you,' she opened her eyes. The pain has not returned.

Chronic Eczema: A woman in her mid-40s was suffering from chronic eczema. She did the one-minute exercise over the ensuing week, and her face cleared up considerably. After a week she encountered a circumstance that evoked her anger, which she could not express — a chronic characteristic. Voilà, an eruption broke out on her face. She recognized the connection immediately, and finally began to reverse a lifetime habit, and begin to understand what she was feeling. After working with imagery and learning to speak up and curb her anger, she was able to substantially reduce the medications she had been taking for the condition."- Jerry Epstein. MD

CHAPTER 10

SOUND HEALING

For centuries, sound energy healing has been used by Eastern and indigenous cultures to affect deep healing. Now, a growing number of health care practitioners are finding it remarkably useful for many chronic conditions, and feel it helps enliven and balance the DNA within our cells.

The late **Melodee Gabler** was an inspired sound work practitioner who gave vibrational sound workshops throughout New York.

"Soundwork works on balancing the chakra systems of your body, of your whole spinal column. It's like you're tuning yourself all the way up to the crown chakra of your head. Many international studies have been done on the benefits of sound healing, including autoimmune diseases. I'm so grateful that sound healing has healed me." *(1)*

Melodee Gabler's call to sound work began with her own personal healing journey, after she was diagnosed with Multiple Sclerosis in 1996.

"About a year after I was diagnosed, I was meditating daily and praying and crying to God to please send me a healer. Two days later a girlfriend I knew called me and said there was a chiropractor in Long Beach named Doctor Steven Angel, who did vibrational sound healing workshops. I went to the workshop and I heard the sounds of instruments that I'd never heard before. I had a healing, an opening up in the left arm of my body that night. I said to myself: 'This is amazing, I'm starting to feel something on the left side of my body' I went a week later to another concert in the city and I heard him again play all the instruments for about 45 minutes.

I went into a silent meditation with his sounds, and that evening I had a Kundalini opening in my body. A powerful energy rising in my body, which went up to the crown in my head. I felt amazing changes in my body. I was able to walk. I was able to sleep. I was not disturbed any more by numbness and tingling. Fatigue went away. I was able to walk on the beach and ride my bike. I was able to actually sit in the sun without getting headaches.

I recently went back to my neurologists and they said, 'You're doing great, you look great, whatever you're doing, keep doing it.' They also did new tests and found no new lesions. There has been no progression of this disease. It was just an amazing miracle. I had my energy back and had my quality of life back as well. Because of this healing experience, I actually began presenting vibrational sound workshops to help other people experience the benefits and power of Sound Healing." (1)

(Note: Melodee regained her health, but died in a car accident a few years ago.)

An Overview On Sound Healing (2)

Sound Work, also called Sound Healing realigns and balances the chakras or energy centers of the human body. The use of sound work goes deeply within the structure of the cellular body and helps us release unwanted blockages and helps restore individuals to an ideal state of balance in body, mind and spirit. In our One Light Healing Touch schools, we include the fundamental teachings of sound work during our trainings. Many of our practitioners have experienced the benefits of including sound work in their energy healing practices.

One of the most important principles of Sound Healing is called resonance. Resonance is the ability of a frequency to set off a similar vibration in another person's body. In the context of human healing, everything in our body is a sound resonator and has the ability to sound outside of itself. By learning to control and direct sounds, tones and frequencies, both practitioners and sound healers are able to stimulate the optimum health of the body, similarly to the conductor of a symphony orchestra. Resonance principles are employed to re-harmonize cells that have been imprinted with disruptive frequencies.

"Using a sound healing tool allows an area of imbalance to be brought back into balance through a 'like vibration,' a vibration that matches the original frequency a given area at which most naturally wants to vibrate. Through the projection of a sound tool's pure vibrational sounds, the waves go to the area of imbalance, and the weak or dissonant frequency is transformed and optimal resonance is restored. I find that Sound Healing, when combined with One Light Healing Touch energy healing, produces some especially powerful results."- Pari Patri, Sound healing practitioner, Clarksburg, Maryland

PHILIPPE GARNIER is an acclaimed Sound Healing practitioner and Instructor who lives, practices and teaches Sound Healing in France and Woodstock, New York.

"Sound Healing affects our three core bodies: physical, emotional and spiritual. At the cellular level, all cells emit sound frequencies as a consequence of their metabolic processes. Further, there is an interaction between the cells' own sounds and those imposed by the environment, including of course sound healing vibrational tools. We also know that sound affects our emotions (e-motion = energy in motion), and we all experience the soothing feeling soft musical pieces have in our mind to calm us down. Finally, it's spiritual, because the combinations of tones makes us drop to a 'still point' from our busy mind which is reduced to the theta or delta brain wave, just like in a deep meditation. This is where the healing takes place.

There's an important distinction between sound healing and music. Music is organized sound that the brain can make sense of. We can easily follow where the notes are going, and expect the next one to be, whereas working with unorganized sound brings the mind to the present moment, to the now, so we're open to receive the energy flowing with the frequencies to manifest a self-healing ignition.

Sound Healing is all about creating a space made of vibrations in a protected environment for the self-healing to occur. And all the beautiful sounds coming from the instrument become a reminder of the healing happening by gently massaging every part of the person in need of releasing.

Sound therapy has been clinically shown to support people suffering from stress-related disorders and chronic pain, as well as patients undergoing cancer treatments.

In Sound Healing, resonance principles are employed to re-harmonize the cells that have been imprinted with disruptive frequencies, and then to send harmonious frequencies to the cellular body as well as clearing the field (electromagnetism) of the body. Sound energy is also very receptive to imagery and the visualization of colors from the practitioner. I often visualize blue for cooling, green for healing, and orange for revitalizing." (2)

Various vibrational tools are used for Sound Healing including Himalayan bowls, tuning forks, crystals or gongs. They each have a specific use and place in a therapeutic setting, depending on the client's condition. Many practitioners enjoy using crystal bowls that resonate with the 2nd chakra (the emotional center); the 4th chakra (the heart and the 6th chakra (the 3rd eye). Crystal bowls have a gentler sound, while the Tibetan metal bowls, if made with the seven metals, have the special value of resonating all-seven chakras at once! Some practitioners prefer an 8" crystal bowl, that is 432 hertz, the harmonic resonance of the planet that they can use for any area of the body.

If you want to purchase sound tools, it is important to experience, hear and feel the sounds that you enjoy. See the Resources Section for a suggested website. When you work with the bowl, you will want to strike it, and then place it next to the body, or on the chakra and allow it to resonate that part of the body. When you get a sense that you need to wake up that part of your body, it's a good indication that working with sound bowls would be an ideal treatment.

Sound work with chanting. Another powerful sound work/ sound healing practice is using the voice, and repeating chants with intention for some duration. This has been practiced in monasteries of all faiths for many centuries. They can be chanted in any language, and chants in Sanskrit and Native American languages are reported to be especially powerful. See Sound work practices for some powerful chants.

Sound Healing with Energy Healing. If the energy practitioner has experience in sound work, they often extol the value of using both in a session. They describe that they first use the sound tools 'to help wake up the body and loosen what is ready to be released,' and then they use energy healing techniques to affect a powerful healing.

Sound Healing Stories (2)

Sound healing has been used for centuries in indigenous cultures to help people suffering from stress-related disorders and chronic pain. Today, holistic practitioners the world over have discovered the healing power of sound and have found success using sound work with patients who suffer from a range of conditions, from migraines to Multiple Sclerosis.

Remarkably, even in the conservative field of cancer treatment, an increasing number of oncologists are inviting Sound Healing practitioners to help their cancer patients, as they undergo the harsh treatments of chemotherapy and/or radiation. The role of the sound-healing practitioner is to use the sound to help the patient release the toxins and residues from the cancer treatment.

Relief During Cancer Treatments

"I scheduled a series of Sound Healing sessions with a client who had invasive breast cancer. She had two surgeries, including the removal of all lymph nodes on the right side and was fearful about beginning five months of chemotherapy and two months of radiation treatments. I saw her weekly through all her treatment. She felt better after every session and felt that the sound work was deeply instrumental in her recovery." - Philippe Garnier, France and New York

Healing from Vertigo

"I sought many different treatments to get rid of my vertigo, brought on by Ménière's disease. I didn't want to undergo the operation my doctors recommended, so I began to seek alternative practitioners. In my travels, I spent time with spiritual healers and indigenous people of the Upper Amazon in Peru, where I experienced the transformative affect of healing sounds. My vertigo was eliminated! I was so impressed that I pursued intensive training in Energy Healing and Sound Therapy." - Philippe Garnier

Asthma

"I worked on a client who had very bad asthma. He was barely able to breathe before the session and during the session, he had to use Albuterol repeatedly. He called me the next day to say that at midnight his asthma cleared and he felt a resonance in his chest!" - Philippe Garnier

Help from Drug Intoxication

"I saw a client who was exhausted and intoxicated from the medications she had to take. I carefully 'scanned' her body and felt the location of the congestions. I then used my sound instruments to bring harmony and balance to her body. The client said she felt immediately energized after the session and felt like she returned to normal!" - Philippe Garnier

Support During Cancer Treatments

"I worked with a client who was diagnosed with cancer and was following the standard path of surgery and chemotherapy. She hoped that the Tibetan bowl sessions might complement her traditional cancer care, and she felt profound changes from each session. She said the Tibetan bowl sessions reduced the side effects of chemotherapy, along with the pain and anxiety generally experienced by cancer patients. It also significantly improved the neuropathy in her fingers and toes. She also benefited from listening to my CD to help maintain a positive outlook through her cancer treatment" - Diana Mandle, Calif.

To Support Natural Childbirth

"When Mary came to my practice she was 9 months and 2 weeks pregnant with her first baby. She said that her doctors wanted to induce labor, but she wanted to avoid taking drugs. I helped her sit comfortably and explained that having a baby was natural, and that her body would know what to do once she relaxed. I told her I was going to give her a sound to help her come into a state of relaxation, and that was just right for her baby to come into the world. I tapped C and G tuning forks (Biosonic Body Tuners™) and brought them to her ears. She immediately took a deep breath, and a wave of relaxation moved through her body. Next, I tapped the tuning forks again and held them over her baby.

She looked like a different person when her eyes opened. Her tenseness and nervousness were gone and she said, 'I know that it is time and I am ready. Thank you." Five hours later she went into labor and had a natural delivery." - John Beaulieu, N.D., Ph.D., New York

To Release Anxiety and Bring in Balance and Energy
"My client complained that she was feeling extreme anxiety, fear, self-doubt and low self-confidence. I began using the One Light Healing Touch Protocols and scanned her energy centers and noticed very dense old energy in her 2nd, 3rd and 4th chakras. As I began releasing these energies, she felt pain in her stomach area. I sensed the frequencies were very distorted and needed to be aligned before I could complete the energy healing, so I brought in my 8" diameter crystal singing bowl. I placed it on her 3rd chakra and allowed the sound vibrations to realign her energy center and bring them into balance. I immediately saw the difference. I then was able to finish the energy healing. After the healing my client said she felt great. A few days later she told me that she felt much more confidence and passion in her life!" - Pari Patri, Sound Healing & OLHT Practitioner

Healing Experiences During Sound Concerts and Recordings (2)

***Richard Rudis's Gong Bath*™.**
In August 2012, Sound Healing practitioner Richard Rudis invited an expert scientist, who worked with a Darkfield Microscope, to study and collate any changes in the blood of selected participants at one of Richard Rudis's Gong Baths™. Richard is well-known for his powerful Sound Healing Gong Baths™.

"The scientist used a single drop of blood from a female volunteer/participant who didn't feel well, and placed it on the

Darkfield Microscope. The blood was tested before and after the Bath. Healthy red blood cells are round. But something had compromised the integrity of the cell walls and 70% had ridged edges and had a roughness to them. There was also debris. Five minutes after a one-hour bath, the Sacred Sound had affected the blood cells showing a great improvement of red and white cells. The red cells were now healthy and round and were less congested; the white cells were much larger and brighter. There was an absence of debris. The blood terrain had opened up allowing the flow of oxygen and nutrients. Detoxification was going on. The inflammation indicator decreased. The immune system was incredibly stimulated. There was a tremendous difference in the blood caused by the healing vibrations." - Richard Rudis, Sound Healing Practitioner

Migraine Headaches

"I've had debilitating migraines for approximately ten years which interfered with daily living. I went the conventional route and didn't get much relief. I went to a vibrational sound concert given by Melodee Gabler, and I was just amazed at the effects. Immediately, my migraines diminished about 90%. I feel more grounded, more centered, more in tune with life, more in tune with my body, and I am very grateful for Sound Healing."
– Anne E. (1)

Stress and Pain Relief and Increase in Well-Being

"My client, Cheryl H, was in treatment for stage four intestinal cancer and was suffering from extreme pain. Just to move around caused taser-like pain coursing through her body. She attended three of my Gong Baths™ healing concerts in April 2018. After the third concert she awoke the next morning free from pain. She said she no longer needed her pain medication

and has been pain free ever since! Her doctors have no explanation."
– Richard Rudis, Sound Healing Practitioner

"I attended Peter Blum's Sound Bath last night. He's more like a shaman than a musician. He artfully danced within his bowls, gongs, drums and assortment of sound, and he brought everyone along on a vision quest, which allowed me to unravel my current stresses and challenges in this world." – Marcella R.

"One of my clients with metastatic breast cancer experienced many positive effects when she attended my Tibetan Bowl Concert. She said her body relaxed in a profound manner and she felt a deep sense of peace and felt that the effects are physical, emotional, and spiritual!" - Diana Mandle, Sound Healing Practitioner

Qi Music

Qigong Master Jack Lim is a gifted music-composer, and he created his popular Qi Healing music to help enhance the body's own healing ability. Listeners report that it reduces anxiety and helps people breathe more easily and feel a greater sense of well-being.

"A physiotherapist from Norway, who has worked in rehabilitation for 40 years, said that she has seen how my Qi music helps small children with severe head injuries wake-up and begin to move their body. The children say that just thinking of the music also helps them sleep!" – Jack Lim. Qigong Master

"My clients use Jack's Inner Peace CD to help them evoke relaxation during childbirth. Not only the mother listens, the unborn child listens too. The baby is learning through the mother's energy field the invaluable lesson of relaxation, and these babies are often born peaceful and serene. After they are born, when they hear Jack's CD, it sets off their own relaxation response." - Diane Gardner, Hypnotherapist, Childbirth Educator, Australia

CHAPTER 11

SELF-HEALING PRACTICES (2)

This chapter presents a range of excellent self-healing practices, and includes Energy Practices, Qigong, Mental Imagery, Heartmath, and Sound work.

All the Practices listed are excellent for helping to attain optimal health and wellness and very importantly, are highly effective at reducing stress.

HYLA CASS, MD. Integrative Medicine expert
"Dealing with stress consists, first of all, of clearing out old programming from our unconscious. Then in our daily life we need to do things such as meditation, yoga, dance, music, all the things that help keep us calmer and more relaxed. That's one of the primary ways we heal our own bodies. Some of the best approaches are: - think positively, eat well, take care of your stress, including very old stress, and live a thoughtful and loving life. I think one of the most positive forces for healing is love and gratitude." (1)

In the holistic field, we call these 'Practices' because in order for them to work, we must practice them! Please use the wealth of contributions that follow and find what works best for you. Begin to develop a lifelong practice and it will reward you a thousand times over! Not only will you benefit - body, mind and spirit - but also all the experience of all those in your life will be enhanced since they will simply feel better in your presence. Remember, we are all radiating 'like little stars' and as we radiate our energy into the world, we can contribute to a more positive and harmonious global energetic. Aim for doing them daily or several times a week for the most beneficial results.

Practices from One Light Healing Touch (2)

Running Energy™ - By Ron Lavin, MA

It is best done while seated, with both feet flat on the floor, eyes closed and feeling fully relaxed. It is ideal to do any time of the day to clear energy and regain our sense of clarity balance. It is on *One Light Healing Touch Journeys* #1.

Running Energy ™ is a healing meditation and visualization. It is best done in the morning, followed by a meditation, then repeated again in the evening. It teaches us how to work with three natural elements: Solar, Earth and Etheric Energies. The practice helps us to release the toxic buildup of emotional stress and traumatic life experiences, helps us to ground, and revitalize ourselves with divine light, as quickly and as often as we choose.

1. Create an image of a cloud above your head. Then take a few breaths and relax the brain and release any stress, tension or fears that you may be holding directly into the cloud. Then send the cloud directly into the sun, allowing it to be destroyed and recycled. Repeat this several times or until you've released all the stress, tension and/or fears held in the body.
2. Now cut your existing grounding cord, imagining it to be like the roots of a tree, going from our feet, deep into the earth. Cut your grounding cord with an etheric knife, and release it into the energy of gravity, allowing it to be pulled deep down into the earth. Next, create a new etheric grounding cord, in any color and texture you chose, affixing it to the base of your spine and feet, and send your grounding cord deep into the earth. Scan your body head to toe, and begin to release any tension or stress. Breathe and release, and send the energies down the grounding cord into the heart of the earth, where they may be absorbed and recycled. Sense the power of gravity, pulling your fear, stress, tension and pain down into the core of the earth. Breathe, release and let it all go. Take your time.
3. Now, when you are ready, sense, see and feel the Divine Light above your head and invite the Light to wash over you, cleansing your aura, and open your crown chakra and invite it to flow through you, filling-in all the places from which you've released tension, stress, pain and fear. See the Divine Light bathing and cleansing every

cell with this healing, Divine Light. Open and allow this energy to run continuously and completely through your body. Breathe and open and receive the light. Then bring your awareness into your heart and breathe and open, and ask your heart for a message. When you're ready, open your eyes.

Meditation – Following The Breath

Meditation is a powerful practice that is thousands of years old. "Following the Breath" is very similar to Vipassana, a Buddhist Meditation. Meditation reduces pain and stress, and improves concentration and general health. It also quiets the mind so you can listen to your own inner guidance and become more present. For best results we suggest you practice meditation after you do *Running Energy,* which enables you to relax, be grounded, with your energy flowing.

1. Relax and sit up, so your spine is straight. Check in with your body, emotions and mind, and if there is anything that is calling to your attention, acknowledge it and let it go.
2. Ground and open your heart chakra and let your awareness drop down and rest in your heart.
3. Slowly inhale and let your breath fill your heart and on your exhale, watch the breath as it disappears. Continue breathing in this way. Merge in the stillness and be in your heart. Before opening your eyes, tune into your heart and ask 'if there are any messages from your inner guidance?' When you're ready, breath out and open your eyes. Try to do this practice 20 minutes daily.

Qigong Self-Healing Practices (2)

Qigong is the oldest branch of Chinese medicine, and is approximately 5,000 years old. The term "Qigong" in Chinese means 'Qi Energy Training.' It teaches that external disruptive influences such as climate, ~~or~~ infection, just the ageing process can disrupt one's Qi. Through the centuries, Qigong has been found-to be a major key in unblocking and promoting the flow of Qi and improving one's health. Today, millions of practitioners the world over use Qigong as their primary choice for self-care practices in order to achieve greater health and longevity.

Body Points and Meridians - It is helpful to know the main energy points on the body to help visualize and receive the most benefits from the practice. The important body points and meridians helpful for any Qigong exercise include:

Yongquan - sole of the foot
Ming Men - lower back
Dantian – lower abdomen, about two inches below the navel
Baihui - crown of the head
Laogong - palm of the hand
Ren Channel -front along center line
Du Channel - back along the spine
Huiyin – perineum

Illustration by The Turning Mill

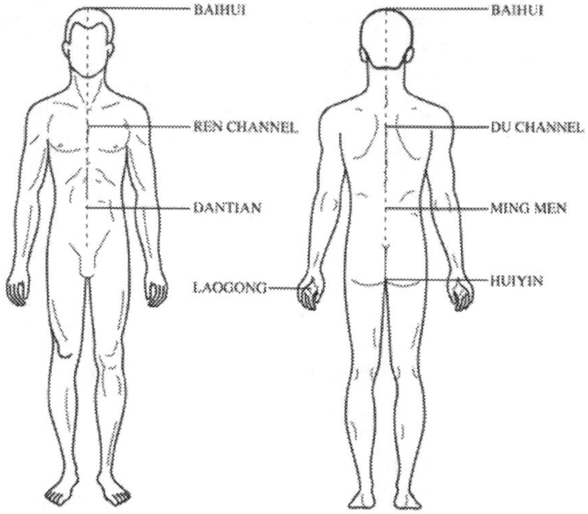

Gary Renza Shares Several Qigong Practices

"Through Qigong practice, we can learn to sense and differentiate between negative and positive energies. Qigong can be hard, soft, quiet, dynamic, medical, religious and martial, but no matter what style you choose to practice, Qigong makes you feel alive and fully aware of yourself and your surroundings for a better quality of life. Along with seated meditation, Qigong can also be a spiritual vehicle to take us closer towards enlightenment and sense of Oneness. Qigong can best be understood by practicing it. Find a competent teacher, dedicate time for practice, and enjoy the journey.

The Three Regulations: *The practitioner must remember to follow the "Three Regulations": regulating the body, the breath, and the mind when practicing Qigong. (2)*

Condensing the Qi*:* This Qigong practice is a powerful way to sense, cultivate and condense energy. When we practice Qigong with the correct mindset, breath control and body posture, we create a stasis within the body allowing for a harmonic balance at the cellular level. This strengthens our internal and external Qi by producing a heat, which permeates outwardly around our body. If left unattended, this energy will dissipate. The practice of condensing the Qi will allow us to will this energy back into our bodies, deep into the bone marrow to strengthen and fortify our white blood cells, boost our immune system and strengthen the bones.

This practice was kept secret for many years. Masters would only divulge this information to select disciples who they felt had the right discipline and integrity to carry on the tradition. Shaman priests use a similar technique in their energy practice. Today, these sacred exercises are now available to everyone.

This exercise should be done after a Qigong workout of 20 minutes or more. To do the exercise, start by standing comfortably with an awareness of your heels and balls of the feet. Feel them sinking into the ground with a strong attachment to the earth. Scan the body from head to toe and try to relax as much muscle tension as possible. Lift the crown point of the head so it feels as if your head is floating above your shoulders, and from your shoulders down feel your body sink, letting gravity root you downward.

Rest the tip of your tongue behind the two front teeth on your upper palate. This will help to enhance the energy flow within the body, and to help the mind from wandering during practice. Close your eyes or rest your eyelids so that you are less distracted by the outside world. This will help you to 'look inward'. Place your hands with your palms facing your body just below the navel. This area is known as the lower Dantian, one of the major focal points during Tai Chi and Qigong practice.

Stand in this position and follow your breath in and out, breathing through the nose. Slow down your breath, making it deeper and finer while maintaining a relaxed state of mind. Now picture yourself as you are standing there and visually strip your body of its skin and muscle until you are a 'living skeleton' breathing in the Life Force surrounding your skeletal body. Visualize this Life Force surrounding your body in the form of a white or yellow smoke or light. With every inhalation, imagine this Qi being sucked into the bones like a vacuum. On each exhale visualize the Qi being squeezed deep into the bones getting denser and denser with each breath. Taking three to five slow, deep, concentrated breaths is sufficient. Next picture yourself with muscle and then skin covering your energized skeleton.

Continue standing for a moment following your breath, inhale and visually circulate the energy up the Du Channel to the Baihui, exhale and down the Ren Channel to the Hui Yin. Take three to five breaths, and then slowly open your eyes at the end.

The Inner Smile: This technique called "The Inner Smile" can be very useful for maintaining a positive attitude and reducing negativity. When you first wake up, make a habit of thinking about something pleasant, something that well, makes you smile. Keep that inner smile radiating in your heart center and keep an awareness of that thought throughout your practice and eventually throughout your day." (4) - Gary Renza

Ken Cohen Shares Three Qigong Practices

He calls his Qigong style: "The Ordinary is Extraordinary" ©.

"Although Qigong began in China, its ancient wisdom is part of the common inheritance of humanity. Qigong is based on the Paleolithic wisdom of our ancestors who were in touch with their bodies and the natural world. The best way to reawaken this ancient wisdom, hidden in our genes, is by practicing the three core principles of Qigong, known as The Three Tunings, three aspects of one's being that must be adjusted and harmonized, like tuning an instrument.

Tune the Body, Tune the Breath, and Tune the Mind

Once your instrument is tuned, you can learn the intricacies of Qigong practice and begin to make beautiful music. Although a Qigong system might take years to master, these principles are easy to understand and can make an immediate difference in well-being, vitality, and quality of life.

Tuning The Body

Qigong begins by paying attention to the body. If the body is tense and the posture is poor, the breath cannot be slow or deep, and the mind cannot be tranquil. The easiest way to change your psychology is to change your physiology.

Stand with the feet shoulder width apart, with your arms resting at the sides of the body, held a few inches away from the thighs. Your arms are relaxed, but not limp. You may also practice The Three Tunings while seated in a chair. Your legs are uncrossed, feet on the ground and hands resting comfortably in the lap. A seated position is advised if you have arthritis in the lower body or any medical condition that makes it painful or inadvisable to stand for extended periods of time.

Keeping the eyes gently open will help with attentiveness (not falling asleep!) and balance. Your eyes are soft, relaxed, and level, that is, not looking up or down. Nor are you looking at anything in particular. Eliminate any tendency to stare. Imagine that you are gazing both inside and outside. Your inner eye is aware of your bodily sensations.

Decide to use the minimum effort necessary to remain standing. Imagine that you are standing so delicately that if a feather lands on the head, the knees will buckle because of the weight of the feather. If a fly lands on the shoulder, the shoulder will drop because of the weight of the fly.

Sink your weight through the feet into the ground. Tension flows downwards and dissipates, like water flowing down a hillside and then seeping into the ground. Your feet are rooted, a tree with deep roots. To develop this rooted sensation, it is very important to consciously relax the feet. Allow your weight to spread evenly through the feet, not leaning on your toes or heels, on the insides of your feet, or the outsides.

Imagine that all of the joints of the body are relaxed and open, never locked. To lock a joint is to close the space between the bones and create more wear and tear, leading to arthritis. Your joints are designed not as weight-bearing structures, but as weight transference areas. And weight or pressure only moves efficiently if a joint is unlocked.

According to Chinese medicine, to lock a joint is to close an energy gate and prevent qi from moving through the acupuncture meridians.

It is especially important to keep the knees slightly bent at all times. The knees are your body's shock absorbers; they absorb the shock of walking on concrete or on any hard and unyielding surface. If you lock the knees when you step, you are jarring your lower spine, which increases back-pain and your chances of injuring the lower back. Similarly, the elbows are subject to injury if you lock the elbows. Imagining lifting a very heavy object with locked elbows. Just the thought is painful. What about the hips? How can you relax and open the hips if they are compressed by gravity? You must use your mind. Imagine that your upper torso is gently lifted up and away from the legs and that you are creating more space in the hip joints. Allow all of the deep muscles that attach to the hips to become warm, open, and pliant. Similarly, use your mind to relax other joints in the body: the toes, ankles, wrists, fingers, and shoulders. Your shoulder joints will open if you say to yourself, 'My shoulders are sitting.' They are relaxed down, neither slouched forward, nor pulled back.

Release the chest muscles by relaxing the ribs and breastbone. Two mistakes to avoid are depressing the chest or puffing the chest up or out. Both interfere with breathing and create imbalanced mental attitudes. Depressing the chest may create feelings of depression. Lifting the chest may make one feel uptight or egotistically proud.

The spine is vertically erect and mentally stretched open and long. Imagine that the tailbone is anchored into the ground and the head is lifting gently away from it, as though pulled upwards from the crown, like a puppet on a string. Or imagine that your vertebrae are beads on a string; the string is delicately stretched to eliminate excess slack. Now there is more space between each bead.

Your mouth is lightly closed, with the tongue touching the upper hard palate. This tongue position generates saliva, preventing the mouth from becoming dry. It also closes a gap between two major energy channels, one that ends at the palate, and another that begins at the tip of the tongue. Although qi can bridge the gap, by deliberately closing the circuit, the qi current becomes stronger and clearer.

Very importantly, your belly is relaxed. You cannot master Qigong if you pull your belly up or in to make it appear flat. A tight abdomen interferes with breathing.

Tuning the Breath

Take a good deep breath. If you are like most Americans, you are probably sucking in your stomach and expanding your chest as you inhale. Yet according to both Eastern wisdom and Western science, this method of breathing is inefficient, shallow, and contributes to anxiety and hypertension. Chest breathing causes muscles to spasm and decreases oxygen delivery to the cells. This can have especially serious effects on neurological diseases, since the brain requires 20% of the body's available oxygen.

To learn how to really take a deep breath, you don't have to read a textbook on respiratory therapy; just watch a child breathing. When a child inhales, the belly expands; when she exhales, the belly retracts. This is the most natural and relaxed way to breathe. To inhale, the diaphragm must drop, opening the lungs and pushing the belly out. To exhale, the diaphragm rises, drawing the abdomen in and gently pushing air out.

Qigong takes diaphragmatic breathing one step further. Imagine that you have an energy sphere in your lower abdomen, about two to three inches below the navel and midway between the front and back of your body. When you inhale, it inflates like a balloon and pushes the lower abdomen out, while also gently expanding the lower back. Belly-back breathing is called dantian breathing. The dantian is the field (tian) of the elixir (dan) of long life, an energy center in the lower abdomen where, through tranquil breathing, you plant and cultivate the seed of long life and wisdom. This method of breathing also moves and massages the organs and connective tissue, releasing tension and improving circulation of blood and qi.

Because dantian breathing is more efficient than thoracic (chest) breathing, you need less breaths per minute to deliver necessary oxygen to your cells. The breathing rate is likely to shift from the American average of about seventeen 17 breaths per minute to seven breaths per minute within just a few months of practice. Slow breathing slows down the brain waves and makes you more relaxed, tranquil, and intuitive.

Tuning the Mind

Tuning the Body and Breath induces a state of quiet awareness of whatever presents itself, whatever is happening. It is not a matter of effort, but rather of letting go, so that the mind returns to its natural state. You cannot try to still your mind, that would be like trying to calm turbulent water by pounding on it. Rather, the mind naturally settles into stillness through self-acceptance and lack of judgment, as though you are saying to yourself. 'I will just let the mind be.' Then the waves of thought cease of themselves. When the surface of a lake is quiet and without waves, it becomes a mirror that reflects the world as it is, without the distortions of thought and worry. The mirror being itself colorless can reflect all colors.

Although Qigong includes many concentration and visualization exercises, the ultimate goal is to move from the particular to the universal, from the state of your deliberate action, to a place of inaction and effortless flow. Rather than concentrating on anything in particular, open the mind to the entire field of perception and being. Ask yourself, 'Can I be innocent, open, and appreciative, without either rejecting or prolonging any thought or sensation?'

If a thought passes through your mind, just let it pass, like a cloud moving across the sky. This state of awareness is called dis-attachment, because you are not mentally or emotionally stuck to any phenomena. When the mind is dis-attached, it is unfettered by memory or expectation, fully satisfied by each passing moment.

The ability to be renewed moment by moment and to see life with fresh clarity is precisely what Buddhists call 'enlightenment' or Taoists–'unity with the Tao, the Way of Nature.'" - Ken Cohen (2)

Jack Lim Shares the Following Qigong Practices for Self-Healing

"The wisdom of the great sage Laotse taught us to 'Be as One With the Universe' and thus, thousands of forms of circular movements in stillness appeared in China following this principle, and so was born the art of Qigong. Through Qigong, one becomes interconnected with the Healing Field of Mother Earth, of the hills and mountains, of the rivers and the ocean, with the great Healing field of the Universe. The practice of Qigong allows the body and mind to stretch out and be totally free. The peace and serenity thereafter cannot be described in words; it can only be felt in person."

The Qigong Healing Walk

The Qigong Healing Walk has been practiced in China for over fifty years. Qigong master Jack Lim reports that it was taught to thousands of cancer patients in China, and after five years of doing this daily, 58 % had no development in their cancer and for some it was no longer detectable.

In the documentary *The Healing Field*, Qigong Master, Gary Renza briefly guides the viewer through the basic steps of this Qigong Healing Walk. It consists of several elements: two short breaths in and one long exhale; stepping with heel down and then rolling through the foot; keeping a soft gaze; and last, on every fourth step, gently alternating the direction of your gaze. The Resources section of this book, includes Jack Lim's website. He offers a free instructional video, *Cancer You Can Beat It!*, which features the Qigong Healing Walk.

Stillness Qigong Meditation

"This practice includes breathing regimes, and helps eliminate the factors inhibiting the vital flow of Qi. Students who suffered from severe headaches, palpitation, high blood pressure, and stomach trouble experienced marked improvement in their condition after practicing Stillness Qigong meditation. It allows for the natural free flow to return.

To practice Stillness Qigong, either sit cross-legged or sit in a chair with feet flat on the floor; the hands are on the thighs above the knees; the eyes are loosely closed and have a wisp of a smile on your face. This smile is very important and if one is beset with great sadness or worry, or is immersed in extreme elation, this is not a good time to practice meditation. Have the tip of the tongue against the top palate, swallowing the saliva flowing in the mouth, down to 'Dantian' where the Qi is. The Dantian is about two inches below the navel.

Clear the mind; gently breathe in thinking of the Qi going down to Dantian, and gently breathe out. Gradually, all sounds and objects around you will fade away. Relax the muscles of the face, then relax the shoulders, the arms, the body and the legs. As you breathe down do not raise the chest but instead let the breath gently push out the abdomen. The abdomen is drawn in as you breathe out. Continue thus from ten minutes to half an hour.

Closing: Now place the hands one hand over each other over Dantian, for at least three minutes, for men place the left hand first, and for ladies the right hand first. Think of the Qi concentrating at Dantian, the energy storage center.

Healing Qigong

After a period of time practicing stillness meditation, you may add Healing Qigong, if you have any part of your body that needs healing, be it for joint pain, muscle sprain, bone fracture, or unwelcome tumors. While sitting in stillness, imagine yourself as a beautiful lotus flower stretching upwards to meet the sun with the golden rays from above shining light, warmth and love on you; while the nurturing Qi from Mother Earth flows upwards from your feet. Be in no haste as you are preparing for empowerment from the Universe as you go deeper into meditation and become 'As One With the Universe' as Laotse teaches us. Then think of the area to be healed being encased in golden light. This is not a prolonged process as it involves a great flash of energy. Now rest for a few minutes. Only do this a few times in one session as it may be very tiring. Replenishing the Qi is necessary after healing and it is described below.

Replenishing Qi

This is ideal to do after completing the Healing Qigong described above, or whenever you wish to replenish your QI. This is also known as **Qigong Earth and Sky.**

Stand and inhale, and slowly raise the arms from the side with palms facing the ground. Imagine pulling the earth energy into your palms. When level with the shoulders turn the palms over and imagine pulling the sky energy into your palms and continue upwards absorbing Qi. When the hands are high above the head, and palms meet, begin to exhale, and turn the palms over again as they come down over the head showering the body with Qi from the skies. Both hands move to the Dantian in the male/female protocol positions.

One hand on top of the other. This is one breath. Breathe normally for three breaths as you send reinvigorating and strengthening energy into your Dantian. This practice will make your Qi power, and your Qi healing field wider and stronger, and ideally should be practiced for 5 to 10 minutes.

Holding of the Pearl for Self-Healing

With one sweep of the right hand the giant pearl is brought up from the ocean and the left hand is placed over it. Both hands then allow the shimmering pearl to expand, and as the hands move outwards many times further and further apart, the pearl expands into a powerful ball of Qi. After doing this for a few minutes, compress the ball of Qi with both hands rubbing them together as the ball of Qi causes tingling and heat in the palms of the hands. Then place the palms of the hands wherever healing is required. Perhaps place the hands near the kidneys over the Ming Men (Door to Life) point for longevity, and on the back for clearing back pain, or cup the eyes to ease eye ailments, or help overcome knee problems with hands over that area. One may proceed with healing other places using the same method.

Movement Qigong - Introduction to The Great Stork Qigong
"This practice more actively clears blockages and stimulates the flow of Qi. Part one of The Great Stork Qigong may be viewed on Youtube. It is best to practice this at least three times a week to bring effective results.

I created this set of Qigong when I introduced Qigong to Australia and it is named after the stork. In China the stork is symbolic of Longevity and Good Fortune and Qigong is known as the Art of Longevity.

Allow this majestic bird to take you to another world as you stretch out your arms mimicking the stork spreading out its wings. You are thus connecting with the nurturing Yin energy of Mother Earth, which flows up freely in the spine. When your hands rise to the sky, you are connecting with the Strengthening Yang energy of the Universe.

When simulating the beautiful graceful movements of the stork in full flight, you are enhancing the circular free flow of Qi energy up the back and down the front, forming circles which in Qigong are called the Cosmic-Orbit. Actually, all heavenly bodies in the sky or the smallest molecules move around in circles.

This inherent circular flow of Qi energy in our bodies is often blocked through physical and/or emotional stress, or through the body's inability to cope with the changes in the weather or climate. The ancient sages of China discovered that all sickness came though the direct or indirect impairment of this most important flow."

Mental Imagery Exercises for Self-Healing

Mental imagery exercises are quite simple and are meant to be done quickly taking several seconds up to one minute to complete. Choose one of the exercises below and do it three times a day (morning, dusk, and before bed) for 21 days, then stop for a week, and repeat again if needed.

Rachel and Gerald Epstein share the following mental imagery exercises.

Sand Salutation - For Energy and Relaxation
"Sit up straight in a chair with your back straight, feet flat on the floor. Don't cross your legs or hands and close your eyes. Begin to exhale through your mouth with a long and slow breath. This special kind of breathing opens the door to the imaginal experience. Breathe in briefly and normally through your nose. On each long exhale, see the out breath coming out as gray smoke like cigarette smoke which you watch drift away in the air and disappear as you're breathing out all the waste products, carbon dioxide, the chronic stress hormones. As you're breathing in, you're breathing in all of the health-giving energy of the universe through the breath which is coming in as a blue and golden light, a light formed by a mixture of cloudless blue sky and bright golden sun as you find yourself becoming calm, quiet, peaceful and in the presence of the moment.

Now we're ready to begin the Sand Salutation. This will help give you energy and relaxation so that you can begin your day and at the end of the workday, it will help you restore yourself and recoup from the day's activity.

On the next long exhalation, see yourself stretched out on a beach, under a clear blue sky, and a bright golden sun. You reach up with your hands and you pull the sun's rays into your solar plexus, which is an energy center. You see the rays coming out of this energy center as blue rays that flow from the solar plexus flowing everywhere in your system. This life-giving light is the mixture of the blue sky and the blue light that surrounds the sun. You are experiencing this blue light everywhere in your being, filling you with tranquil, peaceful, joyful life, and giving you energy, strength, and well-being. Sense and feel what happens. When you're ready, breathe out and open your eyes. (1)

Out of the Shadows - To Improve Self-Esteem
Close your eyes. Sit up straight. Don't cross your legs or your hands, keep your feet flat on the floor, your back is straight, breathing long, slow exhalations through the mouth and brief inhalations through the nose. You're taking in the life-giving, health-giving breath, taking it in as a blue golden light, and distressing feelings are disappearing. On the next long out breath, we'll begin to do the exercise called Out of the Shadows.

This is an exercise to help form new relationships for yourself and to help you find your own power's freedom. Many of our relationships in life are predicated on dominance and submission, where you're seen as a shadow by the ones who are in control or in power. It happens in personal relationships, in corporate life, and in business life. On the next long exhale, see yourself engulfed by shadows. Sense and feel what happens to you when you're completely embraced by the shadows. Breathe out one time slowly and now emerge from the shadows into the light. Let this light that you merge into come over you, around you, and through you, come from above and fill you. Now meet the person or situation that you now feel different about. Now feel that you're in charge, that you're meeting the other in a new sense, as a real person to a real person. Then breathe out and open your eyes. (1)

The Question Mark Exercise - For healing back pain, resolving doubt, or changing low self-image. (2)

Sit up with your hands resting on the arms of the chair or in your lap palms down. Close your eyes and breathe out and in three times, so that you are breathing out long slow exhalations through the mouth and normal inhalations through the nose.

On your next outbreath, see in front of you a silhouette or profile of yourself in the shape or form of a question mark. If you can, notice the look on your face. Now, breathe out one time slowly, and see yourself turning towards you. And as you turn towards you, see yourself becoming an exclamation mark. See, sense, and feel what happens as you complete this experience, and if you can, notice the expression on your face. After finishing, breathe out and open your eyes.

How do you feel? Do you notice any sensations, movement, or changes? Is there anything different about the way you look? Is there any difference between being in the question mark and being in the exclamation mark? Some of you may notice that in going from the first to the second, you become taller and feel lighter, that your posture becomes straighter, that the expression on your face changes from one that may have been gloomy or downcast to one that is brighter. Many kinds of changes may be experienced.

Now, if changes occurred, keep in mind that with this exercise you now have the possibility of making some shifts in your life very quickly. In the course of a day, you may notice changes in your usual response to events.

Beyond A Shadow of a Doubt - Use for resolving doubt and depression.
Sit up with your hands resting on the arms of the chair or in your lap palms down. Close your eyes and breathe out and in three times, so that you are breathing out long slow exhalations through the mouth and normal inhalations through the nose.

On your next outbreath, see yourself engulfed in shadows. How does this feel? Breathe out one time and see yourself emerging out of the shadows into the light. See, sense, and feel the light cascading down over you, permeating and penetrating you. What do you experience and discover? Breathe out and open your eyes. (2)

Beauty - Use for correcting or repairing your self-image.
Sit up with your hands resting on the arms of the chair or in your lap palms down. Close your eyes and breathe out and in three times, so that you are breathing out long slow exhalations through the mouth and normal inhalations through the nose.

On your next outbreath, see yourself as an adult holding the hand of yourself as a five-year old child. Breathe out one time. Have the child ask you three questions and answer each of them truthfully. Afterward, take your child-self in your arms showing it the beautiful surrounding landscape. Then see, sense, and feel this child grow up until it becomes one with you. Breathe out one time. Now, experience the beauty in yourself. Breathe out and open your eyes. (2)

Green Meadow - Use for healing.
Sit up with your hands resting on the arms of the chair or in your lap palms down. Close your eyes and breathe out and in three times, so that you are breathing out long slow exhalations through the mouth and normal inhalations through the nose.

On your next outbreath, imagine you are in a very green meadow on the bank of a small stream that flows fast from a high hill above. See and sense yourself picking flowers in this green meadow. Lie in the grass and put the flowers you have picked on the parts of your body that are giving you difficulty. Breathe out. Sense the sap of the flowers entering your body, rejuvenating and refreshing you with their richness and life force. When they start to wilt, remove the flowers from your body. Stand up and throw the flowers into the stream as they are carried swiftly away from you. Breathe out and open your eyes." (2)

Stress Reduction and Quick Coherence

ROLLIN MCCRATY PHD, Director of Research at the Institute of Heart-Math.
"This powerful and simple technique, called 'Quick Coherence' incorporates imagery, breathing and intention.

We can all take steps to reduce our own personal stress. When you feel stress or-you are preparing for something that might be stressful, it will cut out a lot of the stress. Just take even a minute or two and focus your attention on the area of the heart center of the chest and breathe as if you are breathing right through the center of your chest a little slower a little deeper then you normally would. Really breathing as if you are breathing through this part of your body, the key here is to then activate the positive feeling. So this might be the feeling of care and appreciation that you have for a special place in nature. The key isn't to visualize it or think about it, it's actually to create that feeling that you have when you're in that special place. Those simple steps have profound changes in the way that the rhythms and hormonal systems of our body work, and result in lowering our blood pressure. You'll-be amazed at how much stress you can take out of your life as you start to have more balance and perceptions in the way you handle things and react to life's situations." (1)

Sound Healing Practices for Self-Healing

Chanting is an ancient and powerful practice and is especially healing since the practice vibrates, loosens and helps release stuck energy in the body. So whether you find local chanting groups, or sing at church services, or simply chant on your own, you will find that Sound Work is deeply healing and allows more space in the body for life-giving energy to flow freely.

Sound practice from One Light Healing Touch

NIYEE – Our students love this ancient powerful Native American chant. This sacred chant will help release many lifetimes of energy stored deep in the soul. Begin chanting loudly, then softer, then very softly, allowing the sound to flow through you effortlessly. You can chant for 8 to 20 minutes, as you wish. It is ideal for chanting in groups, or by yourself while driving in the car, walking in the woods, or sitting in nature. The pronunciation is: 'Niyee, Niyee, Niyee, Ho-Wah'

It means, "I release, I release, I release, into the sacredness of the all that is."

***Sound Healing practitioner Peter Blum shares two Sound Healing Practices* (2)**

Toning the Five Vowels Sounds

This is a simple exercise using the voice and hand placement to center and send healing vibrations through the body. It can be done as a solitary practice, or a practice for two people to use together. Tone each sound three times.

If doing this with a partner, sit cross-legged facing away from each other and tone the sounds in unison. Use a cushion to elevate the buttocks and pelvis. Position yourselves so your backs are gently touching, both spines aligned. Make sure the spine is straight and the belly, jaw, and eyes are soft, and the sounds are made with an even, steady, relaxed outbreath.

1. **Sound of U**: Take three deep, slow abdominal breaths, inhaling and exhaling in unison. Visualize a basket or bowl. Make a "U" shape by placing the tips of the middle fingers together, pinkies meeting just above the pelvic bone, thumbs pointing up. Gently resonate the sound of the letter "U" as in the word "smooth. Let the sound come out slowly and pay attention to the energy

in that area. Focus on the concept of 'carrying' - as in what are the major ideas that you carry through life?

2. **Sound of O:** Move the awareness to the area between the belly button and the abdomen. The vowel sound to be resonated here is "O" as in the word-'flow'. Place the middle fingers on the belly button and close the thumbs to touch, making a circle. Focus on a sense of innocence as you tone this vowel.
3. **Sound of A**: Next, intone the sound of the letter 'A' as in the word 'calm'. Place the thumbs together over the heart area making an upward triangle with the tips of the fingers of both hands joining. Focus on the sense of purification as you tone this vowel.
4. **Sound of E**: Next, intone the sound of 'E' pronounced 'eh' as in 'bed'. Rest the three middle fingers of the right hand lightly on the throat, pointing left. Focus on the sense of relationship as you tone this vowel.
5. **Sound of I:** Last, intone the sound of 'I' making the sound 'eee' as in 'free'. Place the index finger pointing up on the third eye area, approximately one inch above the spot between the eyebrows. Focus on the sense of awareness as you tone this sound.

Vibratory Stimulation of Cerebrospinal Fluid

This practice helps to revitalize and repair damage to the body. It is also used as a general awareness and consciousness practice.

Using a large metal Himalayan-style singing bowl (ideally 9-11 inches in diameter), stand or sit with your head upright. Turn the bowl upside down and carefully balance it on top of your head. When it is steady and secure, take a soft mallet or felt and leather-covered dowel and gently strike the bowl on its side. The effect is quite spectacular, as the cerebrospinal fluids are being directly vibrated through contact with your skull and your entire head and ears are in a naturally acoustically vibrant resonating space. If there is an area of discomfort or stress in the body, visualize the sound traveling to that area and revitalizing and repairing the damage.

This practice can also be used as a general awareness and consciousness technique. You can train the mind to focus on the sound as it gradually fades and becomes a more subtle vibration and experience the movement through the cranium and the rest of the body."

Tuning Forks Sound Work Practice from Melodee Gabler

"For anybody interested in wanting to heal themselves or others with vibrational sound, a great tool to use is a set of tuning forks. When you buy turning forks, you'll see that they come in a box. They have notes from the note of C all the way up the musical scale, which also relates to the spinal column, where your chakras are located. It's a great healing modality. The way to use these tuning forks is to strike it until it fades out, and do this two or three times. You can even do it to yourself just by tuning yourself up every single day whenever you like. Just strike each tuning fork until the sound fades out, and it will help balance all your chakras."(1)

CHAPTER 12

SUMMARY, EVOLUTION AND CONSCIOUSNESS (1)

With the dawning of new discoveries in quantum physics, genetics, and the human energy field, we are now seeing momentous changes in the way we approach health care. Countless studies are revealing the remarkable effectiveness of Energy Medicine.

People the world-over are now using powerful energy healing and mind-body techniques for their own health care, to help achieve optimum health, and to bring through the higher vibratory energies of balance and peace. As this empowering wave ripples throughout our world, it can helps contribute to shifts in consciousness and to the evolution of humanity.

BRUCE LIPTON, PHD. Cellular Biologist

"Throughout our conventional science we really emphasize the Darwinian notion that we live in a struggle for survival. A new vision of evolution is emerging that reveals a completely different story. It reveals that evolution is actually based on cooperation, community and harmony. Today in our world while we're seeing upheaval, the evolution that's in front of us is actually one of people coming together and recognizing that we're all part of one giant system called humanity. The human is not evolving, it's humanity that's evolving and it will do so through our understanding of our unity and our collectiveness as one human population."

LYNNE MCTAGGART. Consciousness Expert
"I think the greatest power is the power of unity, and I think many of these modalities in energy medicine teach systems of reunifying humanity and reunifying the world. And that's what we need to do now; that's going to be our salvation."

GARY RENZA, Qigong Master
"Qigong is the study of energy, and in essence that's the study of life itself. Humanity can gain from the practice of Qigong simply by becoming more aware of the oneness between everything, I think with that awareness, we'll have more respect not only for each other but for the planet itself."

GERALD EPSTEIN, MD, Mental Imagery Expert
"There is actually an evolution in consciousness taking place. Mental imagery is part of that change because you realize that you, yourself, have the responsibility and the possibility to change yourself, and you don't have to depend on outside sources for your well-being and happiness. This is the true health care reform."

RON LAVIN, MA, Founder &Director, One Light Healing Touch
"Energy work helps us all better cope with the changing times that we find ourselves in.

It helps us to connect to our own inner guidance, which is pivotal in helping us navigate through this life. Energy work profoundly helps us in this evolutionary process."

BEVERLY RUBIK, PHD., Biophysicist
"With energy medicine we're really touching the closest thing to the soul—to the spirit of humanity. This interest in energy medicine is also contributing to the next step in the evolution in humanity. It is about opening up and using our minds more powerfully in terms of the power of positive thinking and the power of positive energy. If we want to establish a more positive future, then we need to start visualizing and using intention to create that future together. I think we can do that and I think that energy medicine is teaching us how this is possible. And it will be much more powerful as greater numbers reach out and make this shift happen."

More than ever, the world needs us to be our "best selves" in our societies. When we learn to use these exceptional practices and mind-body techniques on a regular basis, we connect with the world in a deeper more meaningful way. As we expand our consciousness and shift our energy from stress and worry, to kindness and peace, we then radiate this higher healing energy into our world. Like millions of little stars, this positive energy will flow into every region, helping people to 'wake up' and live more consciously from being more caring in their families and communities, and being more environmentally conscious, to bringing more balance and unity to our world.

CHAPTER 13

HEALING STUDIES FROM THE FIELDS OF ENERGY HEALING, QIGONG, MENTAL IMAGERY AND SOUND HEALING (2)

Energy Healing Studies

Medical researcher and writer, Lynne McTaggart says in the documentary, *The Healing Field - Exploring Energy and Consciousness:* "There are now at least 150 excellent scientific studies of energy healing and these are those gold standard, randomized double-blind types of studies that are used in science. And they demonstrate a very robust effect and prove without a shadow of doubt that energy healing has produced positive results." (1)

The AIDS Study and Energy Healing Studies

Lynne McTaggart discussed a summary of this AIDS study in the just-mentioned documentary, *The Healing Field.* The following includes fascinating details of the research and the study.

One Light Healing Touch™: Ron Lavin, MA participated in five peer-reviewed and respected distance healing studies with the National Institutes of Health (the NIH), four on AIDS and one on breast cancer. Dr. Elizabeth Targ oversaw the AIDS studies and the results were reported in the *Western Journal of Medicine* in 1998. These AIDS studies have been called "landmark", and are among the most acclaimed distance healing studies to date, and demonstrate that energy healing had positive effects on AIDS patients.

The AIDS studies were double-blind and were conducted through California Pacific Medical Center in San Francisco, and the patients were divided into "treated and control groups." The first three studies were done prior to the development of the "AIDS cocktail". All of the patients in the treated group showed "significant results" and they had fewer new AIDS-defining illnesses, a noted decrease and/or elimination of various opportunistic diseases; lower severity of illness and required significantly fewer doctor visits, fewer hospitalizations and fewer days in the hospital; and showed a significantly improved state of mind and mood. All of the patients in the treated group were better in every way, while 40% of the patients in the control group died. The researchers called the–results "remarkable," since prior to the AIDS cocktail, the opportunistic diseases, rather than AIDS, often led to patient deaths. The results of the first study in 1996 were featured in *Time* Magazine. Subsequent studies were done with more patients, over a longer time, and the results confirmed all the same positive findings.

Patients in the treated group were also asked to keep a journal, making any notes on the day and time, if they experienced any particular sensations during the study, i.e. colors and/or a sense of well-being. Interestingly enough, the patient's notations significantly aligned to the exact time frame when a healer was sending them their distance healing! A final study was done with patients who were on the AIDS cocktail and the results showed that again, all the patients in the 'treated group' were better in every way. After the study was complete, the doctors told Ron that one of the patients he worked on, a man with a brain lymphoma, had a remarkable recovery. They said his lymphoma disappeared the week after Ron completed doing his healings on him. (5)

- **A Compendium Of Studies**: The most complete compendium of studies showing the effectiveness of energy healing is from psychiatrist, Dr. Daniel J. Benor. He surveyed all such studies prior to 1990. They were done on enzymes, cells, yeasts, bacteria, plants, animals and human beings. "Of the 131 controlled experiments on 'spiritual, psychic, prayer or psi' healing, over 50% showed statistically significant results. In 56 of the studies, there was less than 1 chance in a 100 that positive results were due to chance, in another 21 studies, the possibility of chance was between 2 and 5 in 100." (6)

- **A Cancer Study**: Inhibiting Cancer Cell Growth: Spiritual healer, M. Manning used energy healing and inhibited cancer cell growth in cell cultures, producing changes of 200% to 1,200% in their growth characteristics. He influenced them even when he was placed in a distant room that was shielded from electrical influences. (7)

- **Effect on Fungus Cultures**: Ten energy healers inhibited growth of fungus cultures in the laboratory by using intention (sending the thought to retard growth) and concentrating on them for 15 minutes, from a distance of 1.5 yards. The cultures were then incubated for several hours. Of the total of 194 cultures dishes, 151 showed retarded growth. (8)

- **Wound Healing**: A double blind study of 44 patients with artificially created, full-skin-thickness surgical wounds. The treated group of 23 patients received energy healing for five minute treatments. By day 16, 13 of the 23 patients' wounds were completely healed, (wound size "0"), compared with none in the untreated group. (9)

Healing Touch™ Studies

- **Veterans and PTSD**: Post-traumatic stress disorder (PTSD) is a significant problem in returning military and warrants swift and effective treatment. HT™ conducted a randomized controlled trial to determine whether Healing Touch with Guided Imagery reduced PTSD symptoms as compared to treatment as usual, on returning combat-exposed as well as active duty military with significant PTSD symptoms. The veterans were selected at random for six sessions (within three weeks). The results of the symptoms in the treated group showed a significant reduction in PTSD symptoms and depression, and also showed significant improvements in mental Quality of life. 10)

- **Patient Stress/Anxiety**: Patients in an acute care facility that are having an elective surgery often experience considerable stress. HT™ conducted a study with 237 subjects who were undergoing elective coronary artery bypass surgery. They were invited to participate, as either in-patient or outpatient. Patients were placed at random into one of three groups: no intervention, partial intervention, and an HT group. The results of the study showed a significant reduction in anxiety scores and outpatient length of stay by 0.5 days in the HT™ group, compared to the two control groups. However, there was no significant decrease in use of pain medication, anti-emetic medication or incidence of atrial fibrillation. (11)

Qigong and Tai Chi Healing Studies

As Qigong Grandmaster Ken Cohen says in the documentary, *The Healing Field:* "There is actually a database available in English that has over 4,000 abstracts on Qigong research and clinical application. So there are many, many studies that have been performed in the West including the United States and Europe, and of course in China that really prove, that it's not simply a hypothesis that for certain illnesses or certain kinds of conditions there's no longer a burden of proof. We can see extraordinary effects on many disease conditions." (1)

ERIK SKJERVAGEN, QIGONG MASTER, and Mayor of Fyresdal, Norway was involved in a three-year Qigong study in-Fyresdal, Norway, from 2006-2009.

Disabled Workers – Fyresdale, Norway
The government asked Erik Skjervagen to develop a program for disabled workers to help regain their health. The workers had tried almost everything and were given a medical certificate and a disability pension and were unable to work. At the outset, their general health was very poor and Erik was not sure he was able to help them. However, he taught them The Great Stork

Qigong and the group practiced it three times a week, for a total of five hours, and they were encouraged to practice on their own if they felt fit enough.

"The results were amazing. Great achievements were accomplished! 70% came back to work. It took between one and two years to gain this result because of the workers' poor original condition. This Qigong system works for many sorts of problems since it is a system made for balancing the whole body. It has helped people with problems like migraine headaches, digestive disorders, insomnia, and different kinds of pain, depression, infertility, stress and more. The government was very pleased by the outcome and has asked me to continue with the project." - Erik Skjervagen

Qigong Master, Gary Renza says: "In the last 50 years the medical profession has gained copious information about the health benefits of Tai Chi and Qigong. Thousands of case studies have been done, and the most recent study being done in 13 countries where they tested the physiological and psychological effects of Tai Chi and Qigong on the body and mind. Their findings included: an increase in bone mineral density; reduced heart rate and blood pressure; improved balance and stability with a decrease in fear of falling. Case studies indicate that Tai Chi and Qigong hold great potential for improving quality of life in both healthy and chronically ill patients." **(12)**

Mental Imagery Studies

Over the past 40 years, there has been a wealth of research that's been done on the mental imagery process to attest to its validity. This includes its ability to bring changes in the human system, white blood cells, hemoglobin, heart rate, and in various physiological processes, as noted in the studies below. Gerald Epstein, MD has participated in the following Mental Imagery studies.

Mental Imagery Effect on Asthma and Other Factors

A study was done in 2004 to determine whether pulmonary function, asthma symptoms, quality of life, depression, anxiety, and power differ over time in adults with asthma who do and do not practice mental imagery (MI). The study was done at Lenox Hill Hospital in .New York City. Individual imagery instruction was given and they were followed-up in weeks 4, 9, 15. Participants were given ~~7~~ seven imagery exercises to select from and to practice three times a day for a total of 15 minutes. Results: Eight of 17 (47%) participants in the MI group substantially reduced or discontinued their medications. Three of 16 (19%) participants in the control group somewhat reduced their medications. The study also demonstrated that imagery is inexpensive, safe and, with training, can be used as an adjunct therapy by patients themselves. **(13)**

Mental Imagery Effect on Well-Being

A study was done in 2014 to look at the qualitative approach to changes in daily well-being as a function of mental imagery practice. Each morning for a period of one week, participants practiced a brief (approximately 1- to 2-minute long) mental imagery practice designed to facilitate well-being, and after each exercise, they provided brief written reflections on their well-being. Qualitative analysis of these subjective reports revealed significant patterns that correspond to three of the four major components of well-being (positive effect, vitality, negative effect) examined by researchers from a Self-Determination Theory perspective. All participants reported immediate well-being benefits of mental imagery practice, and the changes took place in seconds to minutes. This study reflects a micro-developmental approach to well-being from a Dynamic Systems perspective. **(14)**

Mental Imagery on Heart Rhythm Coherence

This experimental study of 2014 explored the effects of mental imagery practice on psychophysiological coherence, measured as heart rhythm coherence. This state of this coherence is characterized by increased order and harmony in both our psychological (mental and emotional) and physiological (bodily) processes. Psychophysiological coherence is known as a state of optimal function.

A total of 82 undergraduates participated and were randomly assigned to mental imagery, thought monitoring, and control groups. The experiment took three weeks, during which the first group regularly practiced two imagery exercises given by Dr. Epstein, and the second group practiced a thought monitoring exercise. Participants in all three groups visited a-lab twice a week, where their heart rhythm coherence was measured. Results showed significant increases in heart rhythm coherence as a function of mental imagery practice. The effects of thought monitoring practice were much more limited. **(15)**

Sound Healing Studies

Sound Therapy with Cancer Patients

One study looked at the effect of singing bowls on cancer patients. The results showed that the patients were more relaxed and evidenced lower stress hormones, stronger immune systems, and improved quality of life and longevity. The patients were also better able to cope with the effects of their disease and treatments. The study is detailed in the book, *The Healing Power of Sound* by Mitchell Gaynor, MD. **(16)**

Sound Therapy to Rebalance the Nervous System

Dr. John Beaulieu, PhD. and Naturopathic Doctor developed his system of Biosonic Repatterning based on the sonic ratio inherent in nature. He used tuning forks and other sound modalities to help balance the nervous system. He found that the sound stimulates the release of nitric oxide in the body, which is a key component for healthy tissues and organs. He's the author of *Human Tuning: Sound Healing with Tuning Forks.* **(17)**

Singing Bowl Therapy

"Tibetan singing bowls are metal instruments traditionally used for music, meditation, and healing. For thousands of years singing bowls have been used for medical applications but to date, very limited research has investigated the biological effects produced by treatments with these instruments. Not unlike music therapy, singing bowl therapy (SBT) generates live, resonant tones that are both heard and felt by recipients. A study done in 2016 on SBT showed the positive effects of SBT. 'Fourteen healthy participants were recruited to receive a single, one-hour session administered by a certified practitioner. After the single SBT session, there were significant changes observed in vital signs and questionnaire scores of 14 participants. These include decreased heart rate and improvement in MAAS and SVS scores. (Mindful Attention Awareness Scale, and the Subjective Vitality Scale) This suggests that SBT may enhance parasympathetic nervous system activation or dampen sympathetic activation, and may improve dispositional mindfulness and well-being." - Nikolajs Belikoff-Strads, Netherlands **(18)**

CHAPTER 14

RON AND PENNY LAVIN'S PERSONAL STORIES (2)

A Personal Journey of a Psychic Healer

This is an excerpt from Ron Lavin's forthcoming book

Ron Lavin, MA, is an internationally renowned spiritual teacher, energy healer and gifted psychic, with over 35 years of experience. He is the Founder and Director of One Light Healing Touch™, an Energy Healing and Mystery School, with locations primarily in the U.S. and in Germany.

Ron grew up in a middle-class, non-practicing Jewish family in Highland Park, Illinois. His father designed and built swimming pools, and was interested in Science of Mind, while his mother enjoyed caring for her three children. She was also a gifted pianist and was a featured solo pianist at Carnegie Hall in her early 20's.

Ron was born clairvoyant, clairaudient, clairsentient and claircognizant, which means that he could see, hear, feel, and know psychic information. In high school history class, as he would listen and simultaneously tune into the events being discussed, he would invariably see and sense a variety of different interpretations than those that were being discussed.

He quickly learned that 'history was written by the victors and that many history books have little resemblance to the truth. He often felt that he 'was on the wrong planet' and that lying and not speaking the truth was a more acceptable way of being in this world.

In the midst of his inner questioning about the world and his life, Ron had a pivotal spiritual experience when he was eight years old. He stopped by his favorite pond in the woods. He was feeling alone and confused and he opened his heart to God and pleaded. "Please tell me what this is all about? Why is it that I'm not understood by others?" Then in an unforgettable moment he heard a voice that identified himself as Jesus who said: "You are not alone, for I am with you. I have always been with you and I will always be with you. You are loved, and whenever you want the truth, you have only to look within, and there you will find the Truth." "It was very strange being Jewish and yet having this connection to both Jesus and Spirit, so I felt I could never discuss this experience with either my family or any friends. At that moment, I knew the deeper truth that rather than follow established religion. I had found my own real living connection to the Creator Being, and since that experience, this In-dwelling Spirit has always been my guiding light."

During his schooling, Ron gravitated toward business courses because they seemed tangible, with direct, clear-cut rules. He graduated from college with a B.B.A. a Bachelor of Business Administration. After graduation his skills and inner guidance led him to travel to Oaxaca, Mexico, where he started a successful business of exporting beautifully embroidered Mexican 'peasant clothing' for the U.S. market.

While living there, he began working with a mystical Zapotec Shaman woman, where he learned both 'Out of Body' healing work, along with the sacred spiritual teachings.

After Oaxaca, he was guided to relocate and live in San Francisco, California. Eventually, he enrolled at the Berkeley Psychic Institute (B.P.I.), headed by Reverends Lewis and Susan Bostwick, where he learned esoteric Rosicrucian teachings, spiritual healing, accessing kundalini energy for healing, and how to increase his psychic abilities and much, much, more.

In 1981, just prior to entering B.P.I., Ron experienced an explosive kundalini opening, which he later learned to be a profoundly purifying and spiritual experience. At the time, he thought he might have been losing his mind. "I had a 103 degree fever and did not sleep for eleven days. Every time I closed my eyes, I saw past-life death pictures of myself dying in hundreds of my past lives. This experience ranks as one the most incredible experiences that I've ever had! I treasure it as a spiritual gift, and an epic cleansing that would take me through the rest of my life. Afterward, I felt energetically lighter; my face looked a bit different as well and I felt much more relaxed."

Shortly after Ron entered B.P.I., he learned that he had a hernia. A doctor informed him that an operation would cost several thousand dollars, and the hernia could return. Later that day, while in meditation, Ron's higher self gave him guidance that he could sew up the hernia himself, using an etheric silver thread! He did two rounds of this 'etheric sewing,' over the next few days and the hernia was gone and has not returned. This powerful self-healing gave Ron the added confidence to fully immerse himself in B.P.I.as an energy healer.

After studying at the Berkeley Psychic Institute, he began working as an energy healer and became known for his remarkable healing abilities. He also continued studying esoteric, Tibetan, holistic, and Native American Shamanic work.

In 1985, while assisting at a Native American workshop, he met his wife to be, Penny Price, who was studying with the same shamanic teacher in Los Angeles, California. They married the following year.

In 1993, Penny and Ron took a four-month trip around the world, to study and meet renowned spiritual leaders, including Daskalos, 'The Magus of Strovolos,' in Cyprus, Mother Meera in Germany and Sai Baba in India. While visiting at Sri Ramama Maharshi's Ashram in Tiruvannamalai, India, Ron experienced a numinous, spiritual opening and received the spiritual guidance, "to move north of New York City and open a healing school." In 1996, Ron launched One Light Healing Touch, and it is now a respected international Energy Healing and Mystery School, with various locations, in both the United States and Germany.

A Love Story – by Penny and Ron Lavin

Our marriage has been and remains a powerful soul connection for us both, and our life has been filled with deep gratitude and joy.

I was single and working as a producer in Los Angeles, and one morning after I completed my meditation, I asked my eager heart, "Where is my love?" I had begun to feel an electricity and an inner knowing that we would find one another, but I was getting impatient. "Where is he?!" I asked again. My inner voice responded gently and clearly, "There is no reason to wonder or worry. He will be traveling on the same path as you, going in the same direction. All you have to do is look up and you will see him standing there." As I opened my eyes and gazed over the Hollywood Hills, a small feather appeared and landed in my hands! This magical gift allowed me to relax and trust that my love would appear sometime soon.

Shortly after that spiritual message, Ron and I met in Los Angeles at a five-day shamanic workshop presented by a magical Cherokee-Irish shaman named Harley Swiftdeer. Ron had been studying with him in the San Francisco area, and served as an assistant at the Los Angeles workshop. I had been working with Harley in Los Angeles for the past two years where I had the delightful opportunity of being part of his first women's group. Harley had been asked by the tribe's grandmothers to convey the sacred native teachings to women, in the hope that the wisdom could help bring greater balance into our communities and our world.

As I walked into the workshop, Ron's inner voice said to him, "You're going to marry that woman!" I enjoyed Ron's gentle humor, inner knowing and deep calm and ease. There was no pushing, only a keen sense of "being-ness" from him. I had never met anyone like him before.

I recalled the advice some year's prior, from Yolana, a gifted New York psychic. She worked with both the New York and New Jersey police and the FBI. I asked her if I would meet a man who would fill my heart and she said: 'Yes, of course' and she said, I'd know him by three qualities: he would travel to Europe a lot, he would be good in business, and his life was about something for the greater good of humanity. I thought a man having these three qualities sounded quite fascinating, and wondered if he might be connected with the United Nations! During the workshop, I saw that Ron embodied those very qualities, but in his own unique package!"

Ron recounts: "When I met Penny I realized that here was someone who was seeing me in my spiritual fullness, for who I was, as a man, and in a sacred manner. Penny was really there. She met me in a place where I had never been met before. I was struck, as if by a thunderbolt! I came out of that five-day workshop, having proclaimed my love and I looked forward to the unfolding of this new relationship. Being psychic, when I was attracted to a woman, or she to me, I would clairvoyantly 'see' how long this relationship would endure, and what kind of relationship it was. I'd tune into my guidance; and I would get, '90 days,' or 'a great weekend,' or even 'two years'. "And so I was always living in a relationship that I knew had a 'ticking clock.' With Penny, I got this image of a huge mansion, and all the windows on all the floors were brightly lighted, and I knew immediately that this relationship would take a lifetime of deep exploration."

"When Ron and I met, we felt like we had a deep and very old soul connection. I saw at least two past-life experiences. One was Egyptian, and the other was as a Native American.

I experienced the Egyptian vision a few weeks after we met. We were leaving a beautiful Native American art gallery, I looked into their front window and to my amazement, I saw my own reflection, but I was dressed like an Egyptian! I looked a Ron's reflection in the window and he too, was dressed in

Egyptian attire! I was stunned, but I didn't want to say anything just yet. As we quietly walked down the sidewalk, I took my feeling deep inside and asked myself: 'Was this from a book or a movie? 'No' Was it from my own desire? 'No' I opened my awareness into a deeper level of my consciousness, into my very being. Ah, this feeling was very old and it was mine, my knowing of a past life and it felt completely authentic! The visionary experience lasted a few minutes and left as quickly as it came. I didn't say anything, since I wanted to feel it fully, before discussing it, but when I began talking about it a few hours later, much to my joy and surprise, Ron, being psychic, saw the energy move, moved with it and was able to see the same vision! We each described each other to a tee. Here we were walking down a beautiful Sausalito street energetically dressed in our Egyptian past-life garb, walking together in just the same way, arm and arm, no doubt that we had done many centuries earlier. It was and still is one of the most remarkable experiences of our lives. It allowed us to know in a profound way that we were a couple at that time period, and so enjoyed being together that we had found one another again.

I sensed that we had experienced other lifetimes together and so, a few weeks later, prior to meditation, I asked my higher self to show me a vision of a previous incarnation that was particularly meaningful to me. After my meditation a beautiful vision unfolded. I began seeing a Native American scene, which soon became eerily verified. In my vision, Ron and I were shamans in the same tribe. He was male and I was female, and I was assisting him in a ceremony. We were on a high hill, on a star-filled night. The tepees were below, with their campfires sparkling. Ron was dancing around the fire, praying to the Great Spirit, in a trance-like state, and he was asking for some protection and a blessing for the good of the tribe, and he was dressed in an incredible feather costume. I visited Ron in San Francisco, a week or so later and described every detail of my vision for him.

He looked stunned and asked if I wanted to see 'the feather costume' and he opened the door to one of his antique cabinets. He then shared a story that several years earlier, some Native Americans, who were unknown to Ron, serendipitously arrived at his home, knocked on his door, and said that they were guided to his home by Spirit, and were instructed to give him these rare spiritual gifts! When he opened the three brown bags, he found that they were filled with 50-year-old 'ghost dancer eagle feathers outfits', all strung together, to be worn on the wrist and ankles, along with two eagle-feather headdresses. As Ron took them from the bags, I saw that they were exactly like the ones I'd seen in my vision!

Ron proposed to me 20 days after we met and in a beautiful romantic gesture said, "I have come through time and space for you!" Ah, my heart melted and I felt my life unfolding in new dimensions. Our marriage has been a profound gift and joy to us both.

When studying the esoteric teachings of Emanuel Swedenborg, our teachers suggested that perhaps we are 'twin souls.' I've often mused on this remarkable idea when I looked at how many similar incidents and patterns we share, often at the same age in our lives.

We learned that our relationship is called 'the relationship of the future.' It is said that many human relationships are either about repaying a karmic debt, or being attracted to 'their opposite' to learn about those qualities. 'The relationship of the future' is where the care and love the couple gives to one another is equal to the energy they give to something 'larger than themselves,' an idea, cause, children, something for 'a higher good' and for the betterment of the future.

Over the years, my mind and soul have been stimulated and fulfilled by working in the media, helping to bring light into areas that needed attention, and presenting exceptional people and topics that could benefit the public. As a One Light Healing Touch Instructor/Practitioner, I am deeply fortunate to have been guided to one of the most transformative and satisfying healing and spiritual paths I could have ever chosen. This work rejuvenates my body, mind and Spirit, and brings me profound joy when I see how this energy healing work has helped so many. I am also eternally grateful that I am able to share this soul-enriching journey with my beloved husband. I feel that my dual lifepath of media and energy healing are a perfect blend of my heart, mind and soul. It is my deepest joy and gratitude to be Ron's collaborator in leading the One Light Healing Touch schools, where I also serve as Associate Director and an Instructor.

The magic of our union continues to evolve and deepen. We feel the hand of Spirit whether guiding us on an unforgettable spiritual journey around the world, to the spiritual guidance we give our students worldwide, to helping us to find the perfect sanctuary for our home base in Dutchess County, New York. This latter episode caused great consternation to our patient real estate agent, as we relied almost exclusively on spiritual guidance to locate our home.

CHAPTER 15

ONE LIGHT HEALING TOUCH™ - AN IN-DEPTH LOOK AND HEALING STORIES

The Genesis of One Light Healing Touch™

"A human being is a spirit in a body. We already know about being spirit. We're here to learn how to be a human in a body." – Ron Lavin

After a decade of conducting private sessions and workshops around the world, Ron was guided to create the One Light Healing Touch Energy Healing and Mystery School in 1996.

One Light Healing Touch is Ron Lavin's life's work. The school's teachings are based on his life experience, psychic understanding about the true nature of energy, and his Shamanic, Esoteric and Holistic trainings. In OLHT we honor the 'golden thread of the ageless wisdom,' which are the common elements of the four great religions: love, compassion, tolerance and forgiveness. Understanding and respecting the laws of karma is paramount.

Ron also saw that while some people recounted having a few unforgettable numinous experiences in their lives and yearned for more, they did not have the ability, without a mind-altering agent, to connect themselves to that realm. With this work, Ron created a plethora of practices and techniques so students can not only experience profound healing and release problematic energy, and come into their heart, they can also access higher states of awareness whenever they wish.

We tell our students that all human beings can do energy healing and it's like playing the piano. We can all play chopsticks with a simple lesson, but to play well, it takes training.

We see that human beings are like energy sponges. For years, we will hold onto other people's energy, from our parents, partners, teachers, and the energies from old traumas of all kinds, and even from past lives. This makes it virtually impossible to be ourselves; to see ourselves clearly; or to live our deepest heart's desire, since our bodies and auric fields are filled with the energy of others.

When we experience blockages, the first part of us that shuts down is our heart, from an event that 'breaks our hearts' which happens to all of us at some point; then our emotions become shut down, since we rarely know how to express our feelings; so we overload our minds, trying to figure everything out from that one vantage point. This prevents our consciousness from being fully present in our body. Often we'll dwell on the past, with regrets, or focus on the future making plans. Over time we often become numb, sedating ourselves with food, drugs, or being a workaholic, or anything that offers us a way from being present with how we're truly feeling. This disallows us from being fully present 'in the here and now', and from having full lives, personally and professionally.

We found that it's vital to begin by teaching practices, and we offer over 50 self-healing practices, from meditation, movement, breath work, visualization, sound work and sacred ceremony. The practices allow the student's energy to begin to flow. Then we guide them through one of 33 advanced energy techniques and have them exchange healings.

Throughout the training, we teach them to develop awareness using their psychic senses, so they can accomplish a more affective healing. When students work with psychic awareness they not only see and know more about the client's or partner's blockages, but it allows them to connect with their partner's higher self for guidance. Time and again the students invariably say they were guided to 'just the right place' on their partner/client, without a word being spoken. In addition, when we learn to open to our own inner knowing, we then learn to hear the messages from our heart and higher self. When we do this, we have finally found 'our true north' and finding our own inner guidance is an immense treasure.

During this process, the student typically experiences deep changes, from emotional, physical, mental to spiritual healing. Our goal is to help our students develop spiritual autonomy and self-realization, and to help enhance their abilities to know, express and fulfill themselves and to help others to grow and evolve. (2)

In my documentary, *THE HEALING FIELD*, Candace Pert, PhD stated-that:

"Traditional talk therapy is often not as effective, and for deep change to occur, we need to find other ways into the psychosomatic network." (1)

The Dalai Lama has said of all the creatures: "He's most surprised by man, because man sacrifices his health to make money, and then sacrifices money to recover his health, and is so anxious about his future he's not present. The result being that he doesn't live in the present or future, but he lives as if he is never going to die, and then dies having never really lived."

In One Light Healing Touch™ we focus on addressing these issues. Ron Lavin says:

"As students release their blockages and programming, heal their hearts and learn to open to their own inner guidance and intuition, they 'wake up' in unprecedented ways. They feel more fully alive, have improved health and happiness, more clarity about their life purpose and are more inspired to contribute to their world." (2)

Healings Experienced by Students During The One Light Healing Touch School

During the OLHT trainings students often experience deep healing, emotionally and physically. Included below are some students' stories.

Lymphedema

"I had painful lymphedema, which was a swelling in my arms following breast cancer treatments. My doctors said this is a common side effect and that there was no effective treatment. However, when I took the Basic Training, my lymphedema was completely eliminated." – Joan H. (2)

Depression

"I came to the school after suffering for many years with some sadness that I could not put my finger on. I had tried talk therapy, but it didn't seem to really work and I was looking for some other answers. As I went through the school and learned the techniques on how to release old programming, what I found was joy! I continue to use these practices everyday, and all my friends and family have seen a huge difference in me." – Nancy N. (1)

Low Back Pain

"I have suffered from low back pain for a number of years and during the second weekend of the training we did a process where we released a lot of emotional issues, and I felt a shift in my body after that. A week later I went to my chiropractor, and she said there was an amazing shift in my pelvic area, which she couldn't explain, and I have remained pain free ever since." – Joan B. (1)

Chronic Fatigue

"The effects of working with the school have been dramatic. Not only was I able to heal myself of a bout of chronic fatigue syndrome, but I'm also able to overcome some of the panic attacks and anxiety issues I've been dealing with since late childhood. Some of the other effects were that I now feel more connected not only to my heart but to my true higher self. Being more connected to my heart has helped me through a lot of difficult times in my life and given me the guidance to continue reaching for higher levels, higher goals in my life right now." - Ryan L. (1)

Distance Healing on Ex-Husband

"During the Basic Training with Penny Lavin, we were assigned to do a distance healing. I was surprised to be guided to do a healing on my difficult ex-husband. Prior to this we had had no communication for many years. In the healing I focused on his heart chakra and was able to sense the darkness, fear, and chaos that had been enveloping him for most of his life. I sent him white healing light until a sense of compassion filled the area. Four days later, I received an airmail letter from him, and on a single sheet of paper, he had written the words, "Thank You". Something had clearly shifted in him and he connected it with me. Amazing! Some months later, I saw him at a family event and for the first time in my life, I felt a new respect and ease from him. I no longer felt any judgment or controlling energy emanating from him. This unique level of relationship was accomplished without any conversation, and yet it was deeply real!"- Joan B. (1)

Arthritis

"I experienced a remarkable healing on my knees during the first weekend of the One Light Healing Touch School. Prior to that, my knees made noises when I walked up and down stairs. I had seen an orthopedist who took X-rays and MRI scans and he diagnosed the condition as arthritis, and said I would eventually need to have my knees replaced. However, after that One Light Healing Touch weekend, I suddenly noticed that my knees no longer made noises when I walked up and down stairs! Amazing! Today, over a decade later, my knees are still fine. I was so impressed with the work that I eventually became an Instructor." – Karen R. (2)

Breast Cancer And Family Relationships

"When I was diagnosed with a multitude of localized cancer cells in one of my breasts, I was very frightened and was heavily pressured by some of the leading New York breast care specialists to have a mastectomy. Fortunately, I knew the work Penny and Ron Lavin had been doing in energy healing, and turned to them as an alternative to surgery. Enrolling in the One Light Healing Touch Basic Training course, I learned a lot about myself and used the work for my own self-healing. Shortly after the end of the training, I went for a 'check up' mammogram and was thrilled to learn that the cancer cells had all disappeared and my breast condition was now normal! It seemed like a miracle, especially since my boss, cousin and childhood friend all had had what I had, though not nearly as prevalent, and had all undergone radiation; I had no medical intervention.

Soon after the breast cancer crisis was resolved, I had another breakthrough, while visiting with some relatives who had never been especially warm and welcoming towards me. At the end of my visit, I realized I had stopped making them wrong. They may not be the way I'd like them to be, but I do have a relationship with them and it's enough. You can't force people to be what they are not but you can enjoy whatever human connection is there. I have since found a profound new sense of openness and freedom in my life!" – Judith O. (2)

One Light Healing Touch Practitioners' Healing Stories (2)

One of the reasons we teach an abundance of powerful techniques and practices is because we have found that the more the healer is able to clear out, ground, and release their own issues and open to the higher energies, the better the healing result for the client. In addition, it's key for all healers to have done their own self-healing work, before they engage with clients. With this unique training, One Light Healing Touch healers are reported to be among the best in the field. The following are some practitioner's stories.

Clearing Anxiety and Insomnia

"A lovely 80-something widow came to me seeking help for on-going insomnia, anxiety, and fatigue. During the session, she was able to release a large amount of stuck energy connected with long-held sadness and regret around her late husband as well as to unburden herself from carrying a sense of responsibility for her adult daughter's emotional well-being. Several days after the healing, she called to tell me that she had been sleeping soundly, was able to set some boundaries for her daughter, and was experiencing a 'lightness of spirit'. She continues to run energy and do visualizations daily and comes for 'tune-up' healing sessions. She has also recently booked a longed-for visit to the United Kingdom." - Joan Baird, Practitioner, New York

Client with Estranged Daughter

"A client came for a session saying she had been estranged from her daughter for many years, which caused her great sadness. She had recently moved to the area where her daughter lived, but her daughter still did not want to see her. The pain of this sadness was evident in her whole being. I gave her an OLHT Session, clearing her sadness and problematic energy and filled her with light and higher energies to help relax and balance her. Nothing exceptional happened during the session, but afterward she said she felt at ease and content. However, two weeks later my client excitedly informed me that her daughter had suddenly begun communicating with her and now the relationship was happy and harmonious! As a practitioner, I am in awe of the little and big miracles that result from the One Light Healing Touch Energy work!" - Rita Vogt, Practitioner, Germany

Woman with Heartache and Grief

"I worked with a client who had suffered from deep grief and sorrow for many years due to the loss of a special friendship with a man. In spite of being married to a loving man, she still felt a deep grief from an old important relationship that hadn't ended well. In addition, this was destructive and made her feel lonely in her marriage, and prevented her from feeling truly close to her husband. She shared that she had done a number of other therapies in the past, but that underlying sorrow was still there. I scanned my client and sensed where she was holding the problematic energy, mainly in her 2nd, 3rd, 4th and 5th chakras. I began using the OLHT techniques to help release the energies, followed by filling her with the higher light energies.

My client responded very favorably and said she felt a heat in her solar plexus area, which passed through her body, followed by a sense of calm and freedom that continues to this day. She said she experienced a profound feeling of liberation, and was able to release the sorrow that was anchored deep in her heart, and that the dark grey cloud which had hovered over her for-years was now dissipated and she felt a light pouring in.' I checked in with her the following week to see how she was doing and she said that the effects of the healing were profound and that she now feels much closer to her husband, is happier and more able to enjoy the present moment." – Carole Gagnon, Practitioner, Montreal

Patient with Pacemaker

"I worked as a nurse in Intensive Care, and one day an elderly patient who was having her pacemaker changed, was in extreme distress and was highly agitated. The doctor knew I practiced energy healing, so I asked him if he'd like me to do some energy work on the patient and help calm her anxiety. The doctor immediately agreed and I used the OLHT Protocols and directed healing energy through the patient's head into the whole body. The patient immediately calmed down, was fine throughout the procedure, and was clear and calm after the surgery. The doctor had never seen energy work prior to this, but he has since become open to using energy healing within the hospital setting."- Martha S.Bigelow, RN, New Hampshire

Patient with High Blood Pressure

"I worked as a nurse in a hospital and I did a One Light Healing Touch energy healing on a patient who had high blood pressure. They had taken her blood pressure before and after I did my healing. After the healing, the patient's blood pressure dropped by 10 points. (from 140 over 80, to 130 over 80.)." - Nancy McAlley, RN, Belfast, Maine

Comatose Friend in Hospice

"I enrolled in the One Light Healing Touch School in order to learn effective healing techniques in the hope of healing a dear friend who was suffering from 'terminal' cancer. She was in a coma in hospice care. Through the months of the School, I used the energy healing techniques, in addition to distance healing, and I worked on my friend every week. By the 5th month of the course, I received the joyous news that my friend was out of her coma and the cancer had disappeared completely, and she was in complete remission!" – Eleanor D.

Animal Healings

Using energy healing on animals is highly effective. One woman took the course to do just that and after graduation, she volunteered at local animal shelters throughout the area.

A few years ago, Ron and I were visiting a stable and noticed a horse with a 'grapefruit size' goiter. We worked together and did a short healing, following the One Light Healing Touch Protocol, and pulled out toxic energy, and sent in high healing light. A few days later the stable master called us and said the goiter was completely gone! Animals respond very quickly. Cats and dogs often let you know that the healing is done by getting up and walking away! We have many positive stories of working effectively with animals.- Penny Lavin

CHAPTER 16

SUPPLEMENTAL EXPERT MATERIAL (1)

This chapter presents experts seen in the 82-minute documentary as well as other experts whose interviews did not appear in the film. *See Acknowledgments for more information.*

Bruce Lipton, PhD. Cell Biologist
"We are now beginning to understand how our beliefs, attitudes and emotions are actually controlling our genes. Our problem has always been that when we try and get our subconscious programs to match our conscious desires, we don't know how to affect the data in the subconscious mind."

The late Candace Pert, PhD. Neuroscientist

***Cancer**
"Cancer is one of the diseases that is increasing exponentially in our time, which in itself proves that they are not genetic diseases. I don't think people realize how we are constantly making our bodies every moment. It's a dynamic system. That's why mainstream diagnosis is so off. By the time you hear about what it is that you are supposed to have, you know weeks have gone by from the way it was before. We're changing moment to moment and our bodies are very dynamic and it knows what it

needs. If it needs new cells, it will make them. It's changing in response to our thoughts, beliefs and experiences."

*** Molecules of Emotion**
"When we mapped the molecules of emotion, of course we find them in areas of the brain that are associated with emotion. However, our discoveries showed that wherever we have sensory information coming in, sight, sound, smell, taste, and touch, we have receptors mediating emotion. We realized that everything we perceive is being filtered along this gradient of what we're already decided about it. These receptors have also been shown to be the molecular mechanism of memory.

So in essence, it's hard to see things fresh. We're filtering everything through our past experiences, past traumas, and our past belief systems. This makes it easy to get stuck in the regrets and sadness of the past.

The new neuroscience studies are confirming what the theory of the molecules of emotion predicted a long time ago because everything that we experience is filtered through this emotional filter. There really is no outside reality. We are creating our own reality, our own internal dialogues are going on and we're just matching it to what we already believe and think. We actually ignore and forget the things that don't fit in our internal reality."

Larry Dossey, MD, Integrative Medicine expert

***Consciousness, Emotions and Choice**
"We can't explain health outcomes now unless we bring in free will and meaning. A portent example is something that is called The Black Monday Syndrome. This refers to the

fact that more heart attacks occur in the American male on Monday morning around 9:00 AM, then at any other time of the week. This correlates with going back to work, and studies have shown that if people have a positive attitude towards their work, if they have a high level of job satisfaction, if their job means something positive to them, then they are spared the risk of heart attack compared to people that hate their job. So, the question of meaning becomes paramount when you begin to unpack these diseases like heart disease and cancer that kill more people than anything else. What is the meaning of your job? What is the meaning of your occupation? What does Monday morning 9:00 AM mean to you? Unless we take meaning in consideration we can't understand some of the biggest killers in our culture.

We have learned in the past 20 years that people who follow some religion, or spiritual path–and it doesn't seem to matter which one, as long as they pick one and stick with–it– are generally healthier. They often have good health habits, may drink and smoke less, often have rich social structures, and have a positive sense of meaning and purpose. We have found that they both live longer and have a lower instance of all the major diseases. For all these reasons, I think spirituality and religion should be part of the factors that we think about in terms of how to improve health, because they definitely have a profound effect on health and longevity."

***Premonitions and Our Health**

"I have researched premonitions and I have decided they are a kind of a preventive medicine, because many people's premonitions warn them of health challenges. It may even save their life. Almost everybody has a story they can share, from an approaching traffic accident, an accident around the home, a breast lump, that they didn't know about before they had a premonition. All of these things have a health influence. I think this ability to intuit is a great gift, because it certainly adds to our longevity if we take them seriously."

Rollin McCraty, PhD., Director of Research, at the Institute of HeartMath

***Quantum Systems**

"One of the greatest discoveries out of the last hundred years of research is the understanding that the universe itself is coherent and holistic and everything is connected to everything else. This is the field of quantum physics and it gives us new understanding about health and wellness, since our biological systems are actually quantum coherent systems. What's become very clear is that our social connectedness is a more powerful influence on our health than a lot of the standard risk factors. Even our social systems are embedded within the planetary system, and a surprising amount of research shows that the planetary fields profoundly affect human health and behavior on a mass scale."

Beverly Rubik, PhD. Biophysicist

***The Effectiveness of Energy Medicine**

"Energy medicine is a huge field and includes a number of different modalities such as energy healers, and people who are using various consumer devices and modalities such as homeopathy, magnet healing, light therapy, sound therapy, visualizations and tapping. It's more powerful than just talk therapy. People are also finding that these modalities are gentler, safe and effective and are helping them feel better, by alleviating their pain, improving their moods and without the drug side effects. When a person suffers a trauma there are often lasting effects wither it's a shell shock from war in Iraq or a violent incident at home. Energy medicine can be very helpful for these traumas and in the healing they move to a new mode of accepting that trauma and moving beyond it. They don't go back to the pre-state before the trauma. They move to a new dynamic mode, and the biofield helps them orchestrate this since it makes the new dynamics come together."

Lynne McTaggart, Consciousness Expert

*** How Meditation Affects the Brain.**

"There is a vast body of evidence about the positive effects of meditation: anything from advanced immune response, to lowering pain, to nervous system responses, to a better functioning heart and even improved-eyesight. But now the latest evidence has looked at the effect of meditation on the brain, and it has found how profound the effect of thoughts is and how thoughts change the brain. They've shown for instance that when Buddhist monks think certain compassionate thoughts about the world, it enhances that part of the brain with happy thinking and positivity. They have a happier brain. They've also found that just a few weeks of meditation can enlarge certain structures of the brain and connect the emotion and the cognitive parts of the brain together. They create a better pathway between our intuitive senses and our cognitive senses which balances the brain. So what we're really saying is that thinking certain thoughts changes the structure of the brain.

There was an amazing study done that looked at Buddhist monks in a freezing monastery in winter. They were wrapped in freezing wet sheets and were only clothed in light clothes. Ordinarily this kind of situation would create hypothermia in very short order and we would lose consciousness. However, the monks didn't shiver, and they began to sweat! They had gotten into a meditative brain state where they increased their body temperature by something like 17 degrees turning themselves in a sense into a human furnace. So what this demonstrated is the enormous power of thinking, and that thinking certain thoughts can change our physicality to that extent.

There are a number of modern studies being carried out in neuroscience laboratories around America demonstrating that even a few weeks of thinking a certain thought such as compassionate meditation or even just ordinary meditation actually changes the structure of the brain and enlarges certain portions. People who get involved in a certain type of meditation requiring a lot of attention increase the size of the brain involved in attention. People who spend a lot of time meditating on compassion increase the happiness portion of the brain and also the portion of the brain involved in helping people. These kinds of studies point to the fact that our brain is highly plastic and can change and revise itself throughout life.

***The "Placebo Effect"**

"Doctors complain about the placebo effect because they say it messes up drug studies. The placebo effect is probably the most powerful medicine we have. It works about 60-70% of the time. And what it demonstrates is that as far as our bodies and our brains are concerned, we can't distinguish between a chemical and the thought of a chemical, the thought of a medicine. There have been a couple of really fascinating studies about this. In one heart medicine study which included 46,000 people, they found there was no difference in patients who have been given a placebo and patients who were given the actual drug. But what was really fascinating about it was that either patient taking a placebo or a drug got better so long as they followed the instructions about the drug to the letter. The patients that didn't follow orders were the ones who got ill. What this suggests is when somebody really believes they're taking a drug, it doesn't really matter in a sense if they're really taking the drug or just a sugar pill.

***The Zero Point Field**

Einstein said the field is the only reality, and it was quite wise because of what matter actually is. When we think of things out there, we think of discreet objects including ourselves. We think we end with the hair on our skin and at which point the rest of the universe begins, but actually subatomic particles trade energy back and forth like an endless game of tennis. All subatomic particles engage in this kind of trade and they create what's called a little virtual particle that has a tiny bit of energy and it's there for less than a blink of an eye. So all the bits of matter and all the things in the universe add up to an enormous amount of energy happening there in space. This gives rise to a quantum energy field known by physicists as the zero point field. They call it zero point because it still occurs even in very cold temperatures approaching absolute zero. What this means is that we're part of this enormous energy field and that when we think of a thing, it's actually a dynamic batch of energy being traded within this field back and forth endlessly. So within every moment you're a different set of subatomic particles in a sense with every breath you take.

*** Remote Viewing**

"The late Ingo Swan was one of the most famous remote viewers and he was even involved with a special CIA program that was attempting psychic spying on the Russians in the-1960s. Swan was born with a particular gift, the ability to see things beyond the-five senses. So if you gave him a set of coordinates on a map he could actually view what was there without being present. He could see something inside a closed box or across the street or in the next country. Now what we're finding is that everybody has the ability to remote view. Certain people have a gift, just like somebody who plays the piano very well, but everybody has that capacity. And we can all learn how to do it and just become better with practice."

ENDNOTES AND STUDIES

Endnote 1: Chapters 1-12 & 16: Quoted material is from interviews conducted for the documentary, *The Healing Field*, 2010-2013. It includes experts seen in the 82-minute film as well as other experts whose interviews did not appear in the film.
See Acknowledgments and Resources sections.

Endnote 2: Chapters 7-11, 13,14,15: Quoted material was obtained through interviews and experts' contributions to the author in 2018-19.
See Acknowledgments and Resources sections.

Endnote 3: Chapter 7: Energy Healing:
Master Healer Energy: M. Conner, G. Schwartz, et al. – Research paper presented at the *Toward a Science of Consciousness seminar* – Tucson, Arizona, April 2006.

Endnote 4: Chapter 11: Healing Practice: Qigong:
Inner Smile - A Comprehensive Review of Health Benefits of Qigong and Tai ChI- Roger Jahnke, OMD Linda Larkey, PhD, Fang Lin

Endnote 5: Chapter 13: Energy Healing:
AIDS Study: Fred Sicher, MA; Elizabeth Targ, M.D.; Dan Moore, Ph.D.; Helene Smith, Ph.D., "A Randomized Double-Blind Study of the Effect of Distant Healing in a Population with Advanced AIDS", *The Western Journal of Medicine*, Volume 169, number 6. (Dec. 1998): 356-363. The sponsors of

the study included: Elizabeth Targ, MD, and The Institute for Noetic Sciences.

Endnote 6: Chapter 13: Compendium of Studies:
Medical Surveys And Research Books on Energy Healing: Dr. Daniel J. Benor, "Survey of Spiritual Healing Research" *Journal of Complementary Medical Research* (1990) and his book, *Healing Research* (Munich: Helix Verlag GmbH, 1993) Address: Windeckstr. 82, D-81375 Munich, Germany.

Endnote 7: **Chapter 13:** Inhibiting Cancer Cell Growth, by Spiritual Healer, M. Manning: W. G. Braud, G. Davis and R. Wood, "Experiments with Matthew Manning" *Journal of the American Society for Psychical Research* 50, no. 782 (1979): 199-223

Endnote 8: **Chapter 13:** Energy Effects On Fungus: J. Barry, "General and Comparative Study of the Psychokinetic Effect on a Fungus Culture." *Journal of American Parapsychology* 32 (1968): 237-43

Endnote 9: Chapter 13: Wound Healing, TT Study: Daniel P. Wirth, "The Effect of Non-Contact Therapeutic Touch on the Healing of Full Thickness Dermal Wounds," *Subtle Energies* 1:1, 1-20

Endnote 10: Chapter 13: Veterans And PTSD; Jain, S., McMahon, G.F., Hasen, P., Kozub, M.P., Porter, V., King, R. & Guarneri, E.M. (2012). Healing Touch with Guided Imagery for PTSD in returning active duty military: A randomized controlled trial. *Military Medicine*, 177 (9), 1015-1021.

Endnote 11: Chapter 13: Patient Stress & Pain: MacIntyre, B., Hamilton, J., Fricke, T., Ma, W., Mehle, S., & Michel, H. (2008). "The efficacy of Healing Touch in coronary artery bypass surgery recovery", a randomized clinical trial, *Alternative Therapies*, 14(4), 24-32.

Endnote 12: Chapter 13: Qigong
A Comprehensive Review Of Health Benefits Of Qigong And Tai Chi - Roger Jahnke, OMD Linda Larkey, PhD, Fang Lin

Endnote 13: Chapter 13: Mental Imagery
Epstein, Gerald N., James P. Halper, Elizabeth Ann Manhart Barrett, Carole Birdsall, Monnie McGee, Kim P. Baron, and Stephen Lowenstein. "A Pilot Study of Mind–Body Changes in Adults with Asthma who Practice Mental Imagery." *Alternative Therapies in Health and Medicine* 10, no. 4 (July & Aug. 2004): 66-71. Accessed March 6, 2018.

Endnote 14: Chapter 13: Kaplan, Ulas, Gerald N. Epstein, and Anne Sullivan Smith. "Microdevelopment of Daily Well-Being through Mental Imagery Practice." *Imagination, Cognition and Personality* 34, no. 1 (October 10, 2014): 73-96. Accessed March 6, 2018. doi:10.2190/ic.34.1.f.

Endnote 15: Chapter 13: Kaplan, Ulas, and Gerald N. Epstein. "Psychophysiological Coherence as a Function of Mental Imagery Practice." *Imagination, Cognition and Personality* 31, no. 4 (November 01, 2012): 297-312. doi:10.2190/ic.31.4.d.

Endnote 16. Chapter 13: Sound Healing
From the Book: *The Healing Power of Sound: Recovery from Life-Threatening Illness Using Sound, Voice, and Music* - by Dr. Mitchell Gaynor

Endnote 17: **Chapter 13**. From the Book: The Med Pub Abstract which can be found in the back of Dr. Beaulieu's book, *Human Tuning: Sound Healing with Tuning Forks* - by Dr. John Beaulieu

Endnote 18: Chapter 13: Singing Bowl Therapy Study Portland, Oregon
Nikolajs Belikoff-Strads, ND, MSiMR, Naturopathic Doctor and Research Scientist
Nikolajs did the study in 2016 for his thesis at the Helfgott Research Institute, National University of Natural Medicine, Portland, Oregon.

ACKNOWLEDGMENTS AND RESOURCES

My gratitude goes to the following people for their expertise, kindness and generosity of spirit in contributing their time and knowledge to this book.

General Experts

Hyla Cass, MD is a psychiatrist and leading expert in Integrative Medicine. She is the author of more than 10 popular books including, *8 Weeks to Vibrant Health.*
California www.cassmd.com

Larry Dossey, MD is a distinguished expert in Integrative Medicine. He is the author of 11 books, including *One Mind* and the best-seller, *Healing Words.* He lectures at medical schools and hospitals throughout the country. www.dosseydossey.com

Bruce Lipton, PhD is a pre-eminent scientist in the field of quantum physics, DNA and stem cell biology. He is the author of two books, *Spontaneous Evolution* and the bestseller, *The Biology of Belief.* California. www.brucelipton.com

Rollin McCraty, PhD is Director of Research of the Institute of HeartMath and is the coauthor *of The Coherent Heart.* The Institute is one of the leading organizations devoted to understanding the physiology of stress, heart-brain interactions and performance. www.heartmath.com

Lynne McTaggart is a preeminent spokesperson on consciousness and the new physics. She is an award-winning author of six books including the bestsellers, *The Field* and *The Intention Experiment.* United Kingdom. www.lynnemctaggart.com

The late **Candace Pert, PhD** was an internationally recognized neuroscientist and pharmacologist and expert in mind-body medicine. She is the author of *Molecules of Emotion.*

Beverly Rubik, PhD is a Biophysicist and is the President of the Institute for Frontier Science. She is renowned for her countless studies concerning energy medicine. San Francisco, California

One Light Healing Touch™ Instructors and Energy Practitioners

Ron Lavin, MA is the founder and director of One Light Healing Touch, an International Energy Healing and Mystery School. Lagrangeville, NY. He's also the creator of an audio series, One Light Healing Touch Journeys.

Penny Lavin is the Associate Director and a One Light Healing Touch Instructor/practitioner. Lagrangeville, New York. www.OLHT1.com

Julia Ananda is a One Light Healing Touch Instructor/practitioner who integrates yoga therapy with her work. Salt Lake City, Utah. www.freetobefree.com

Joan Baird, LCSW-R is a One Light Healing Touch Practitioner and employs sound work in her healing practice. She is a long time yoga practitioner and is a retired licensed clinical social worker. Brewster, New York. www.joanbairdhealing.com

Angelica Bingenheimer is a One Light Healing Touch Instructor/practitioner and teaches the *Healing Hands* workshops in Germany. Angelica is also a GP and homeopath. Jugenheim, Germany. www.bingenheimer-arzt.de

Joachim Deschermaier is a One Light Healing Touch Instructor/practitioner, an osteopath and alternative practitioner. Mainz and Munich, Germany. www.spirituelle-lebenspraxis.de

Carole Gagnon is a One Light Healing Touch Practitioner, a yoga and meditation teacher, and wellness coach. Montreal, Canada. facebook.com/carole.gagnon

Lyn McGuffey is a One Light Healing Touch Instructor/Practitioner and employs sound work in her practice. Indianapolis, Indiana. www.Lynmcguffeyhealing.com

Karen Ransom is a One Light Healing Touch Instructor/practitioner and a licensed massage therapist. Rhinebeck, New York. www.rhinebeckbowenwork.com

Jennifer Schnabel is a One Light Healing Touch Practitioner and is studying aromatherapy. Syracuse, NY. www.alternativehealinginc.com

And **One Light Healing Touch Practitioners**: Martha Sullivan Bigelow, RN, Surry, New Hampshire; Nancy McAlley, RN, Belfast, Maine; Rita Vogt, physician, Freiburg, Germany; Mary Kay McGraw, LMT, Albany, NY (albanyonenesshealingarts.com); and graduate Judith Oringer.

Healing Touch™ Practitioner

Linnie Thomas, HTCP, HTCI, MLW, is an Instructor/practitioner with the Healing Touch Program™. She has authored numerous books, including *The Encyclopedia of Energy Medicine*. Linnie conducts workshops and lectures about energy medicine and spirituality. Tualatin, Oregon. www.linniethomas.com

Qigong Practitioners

Anthony Barker is a Qigong Master and teacher. He has studied The Great Stork Qigong and Healing Sounds with Jack Lim since 1994, has worked with Qigong Masters in China, and organizes Qigong trips to China and Melbourne, Australia. Facebook: MorningtonPeninsuladiversewellness

Glenda Channels is a Qigong Master, Counselor and Family Therapist, Melbourne, Australia.

Richard Clegg is a Qigong Teacher/ Qigong Therapist and an Integrative Therapist using Medical Qigong. He specializes in using Qigong to heal the root issues of people's disease or disharmony at the level of mind, body and spirit. He offers in-person and distance healing sessions. Poughkeepsie, New York. www.laohulonghealth.com

Kenneth Cohen is a renowned Qigong and Tai Chi Grandmaster and has been practicing these arts for more than 50 years. He is the author of many books and CDs., including the bestseller *The Way of Qigong.* Ken offers classes and a Teacher Training program, Boulder, Colorado and San Diego, California. www.qigonghealing.com

Jack Lim is a preeminent Qigong Grandmaster and author of his popular DVD, *The Great Stork Qigong.* He teaches The Great Stork Qigong and Qi healing. He spreads healing through his Qi Energy music and offers his Qi Energy Music CD sampler for free. Melbourne, Australia. www.relaxationmusic.com.au

Sifu Gary Renza is a Tai Chi/ Qigong /Kung Fu Master and an herbalist, writer and lecturer. Cold Spring, New York. www.hudsonvalleymartialarts.org

Erik Skjervagen is a Qigong Grand Master, acupuncturist, economist and the Mayor of Fyresdal, Norway.

Mental Imagery Practitioner

The late **Gerald Epstein, MD** was a renowned mental imagery expert and has authored many books and CDs, including the bestseller *Healing Visualizations.* His wife and longtime collaborator, Rachel Epstein, co-authored Jerry's final book, *We Are Not Meant to Die*, and she continues teaching this work. Rachel Epstein L.Ac. is the Director of The American Institute for Mental Imagery (AIMI) and maintains a private imagery practice. New York, NY. www.drjerryepstein.org

Sound Healing Practitioners

John Beaulieu is a Naturopathic physician, a psychologist and a renowned composer musician, artist, poet and healing artist. He is the author of numerous books including *Music and Sound in Healing Arts*, and *Human Tuning: Sound Healing with Tuning Forks.* Stone Ridge, New York. www.johnbeaulieu.com

Peter Blum is an Interfaith Minister and hypnotherapist and has studied music and sound healing for many years. He has given sound healing concerts throughout the New York area, including at the United Nations. He is deeply interested in the effects of music and sound on physical, mental, emotional and spiritual health. Woodstock, New York. www.soundsforhealing.com

The late **Melodee Gabler** was a Sound Work practitioner who presented Vibrational Sound workshops in Long Beach, New York.

Philippe Garnier is a highly accomplished sound healing teacher and practitioner. He is trained in energy healing, sound therapy and in a variety of Native traditions and sacred ceremony. He created and teaches at the Sound Healing Training programs at the Sage Academy in Woodstock, New York and the Academy of Sonotherapy in France.
www.academiedesonotherapie.com (La Pradet, France)
www.sageacademyofsoundenergy.com (Woodstock, New York)

Mitchell Gaynor, MD is an oncologist at Weill Cornell Medical College Center for Integrative Medicine in New York and is a sound practitioner. He studied the use of singing bowls on his cancer patients and found they were better able to cope with the effects of their disease and cancer treatments. He is the author of *The Healing Power of Sound.*

Diane Mandle is a brilliant author, recording artist, Tibetan Bowl practitioner, and educator. She presents educational concert programs around the world, and owns and operates the Tibetan Bowl Sound Healing School. Diane was part of the integrative therapy team at the San Diego Cancer Center and is the author of the award-winning book, *Ancient Sound for a New Age.* Encinitas, California www.soundenergyhealing.com

Pari Patri is an accomplished sound healer who also works with energy healing, crystals, pyramids, and meditation. She is also a OLHT Practitioner and is Pres. of the Pyramid Spiritual Societies Movement. Clarksburg, Maryland. www.paripatri.com

Richard M. Rudis has studied Eastern philosophy for thirty years and has been teaching Buddhist Dharma via "Vibrational Sound Healing Workshops' since 1988. He is an author, musician and lecturer on the subject of sacred sound healing and how it is reflected within the Tibetan Buddhist tradition and current scientific understanding. He conducts sound healing experiences known as a 'Gong Bath™' nationally and has produced sound healing CDs/DVDs. Encinitas, California www.sacredsoundgongbath.com

Nikolajs Belikoff-Strads, ND, MSiMR, is a Naturopathic Doctor and Research Scientist. He did the study on Singing Bowl Therapy described in the chapter on Sound Healing. He is in the process of becoming certified in Tibetan Sound Healing. Portland, Oregon

ADDITIONAL RESOURCES

THE FILM: ***THE HEALING FIELD*** - *Exploring Energy & Consciousness* by filmmaker, Penny Price Lavin. It is available on Amazon, Beyondword.com, and Gaia.com. Gaia.com carries the 60-minute version, where it can be seen in English, German, French and Spanish. The 82 minute full-length DVD can be streamed and purchased from Amazon and Beyondword.com

Author, Penny Price Lavin: OLHT1.com • pennypricemedia.com. (Lagrangeville, New York)

Sound Healing resources
www.silverskyimports.com (They sell good quality metal and crystal-bowls)
www.soundhealingcenter.com
SoundhealingResearchfoundation.org (California)

Health websites resources
www.mercola.com (Excellent for research on any health topic)
www.terrywahls.com (Terry Wahls, MD, developed an easy, sensible diet to reverse her multiple sclerosis and help treat all chronic autoimmune conditions.)
www.healthadvocatesworldwide.com (A health advocacy group for natural and alternative health, specializing in ALZ, ALS.)
www.peterrussell (Renowned expert on consciousness, eastern philosophy and meditation.)
Prescription for Nutritional Healing. By Balch and Balch, MD (A Reference Guide to Natural Remedies)

APPENDIX

The One Light Healing Touch™ Program (OLHT1.com)

One Light Healing Touch offers a comprehensive program for students who seek deep personal healing, body, mind and spirit, and for those who wish to become accomplished energy healing practitioners. It serves the novice and advanced energy practitioner alike and honors all spiritual traditions. Many of the One Light Healing Touch techniques work on deep subconscious levels to release long-held blockages and programming. This allows students and clients to experience transformational and lasting change on physical, emotional and spiritual levels.

The schools are primarily located in the U.S. and Germany and recent trainings have been scheduled in London. The OLHT programs include workshops, private sessions and an energy healing school consisting of a Basic, Masters and Teacher Training programs. The Basic is 12-18 days and is presented over a number of months. Each instructor schedules their schools based on their own needs. The Masters is 8-10 days and is offered every few years.

All locations and school schedules are listed on the Calendar page on the website.

For in-person and distance healing sessions, see our list of Certified Practitioners.

The One Light Healing Touch Program includes:

- Training in seven of the recognized CAM ("Complementary and Alternative") practices: Long Distance Healing, Energy Healing, Guided Imagery, Healing Movement, Meditation, Mind-body Healing, Non-religious Spirituality.
- The Basic Training teaches over 50 shamanic, holistic, spiritual self-healing practices, including movement, meditation, sound work, sacred ceremony, breath work and visualizations.
- The Nine-Point Protocol™, which ensures that healings are done in a safe and ethical manner.
- The Basic Training teachers 33 advanced energy healing techniques that help people release long-held programming and subconscious energy for healing oneself and others, including: radiant, color, heart healing, male/female work, chakras, chelation, spiral healing, long distance, past life, time line healing, archangelic, white light, Supreme Being, shamanic, and many more.
- The Masters program includes Kundalini healing, Akashic Records, working with your Infinite Soul, crystals, sound work, shamanic work, and more.
- Practices and techniques to increase one's health, awareness, joy, creativity, intuition and other psychic abilities, deepen one's spiritual connection and help reveal one's purpose for being in this lifetime.
- Practices to open to one's inner guidance and higher self, to develop clairvoyance, intuition and other psychic senses and for guidance during the healing process.

- Powerful heart-healing techniques, essential to one's growth and opening to spirit.
- It has been approved for continuing education credits for massage therapists.

ABOUT THE AUTHOR

Penny Price Lavin
The Author's Journey: Opening to Inner Guidance and Energy Healing

As mentioned, my life journey has always been two fold: to bring in light and healing both through the media and energy healing work. I was brought up in an upper-middle class Philadelphia family with four siblings. In elementary school, my love of media manifested when I started a little newspaper, which my best friend and I co-wrote and distributed to our supportive family and neighbors. My beautiful, loving mother was a nurse and an artist. My charismatic father was a brilliant lawyer, who was awarded "Man of the Month" by the Philadelphia Chamber of Commerce.

My family was Episcopalian, but my interest in spirituality began when I had a personal experience of reincarnation when I was eight years of age. One day after a church service, on my way downstairs to the children's classrooms, I stopped on the landing and felt a powerful surge of energy pass through my body. I felt a sense of timelessness and I began to hear my inner voice for the first time in my life. I looked at each of my childhood friends, and I sadly and intuitively knew that I would never really know what it would be like to be any one of them in this lifetime, but that I would only know my own experience of life from the part of me that looked out from 'behind my eyes.' I was acutely aware that my inner guidance said, 'in this lifetime' which was a new concept to my 8 year-old self!

I felt that part of me, that was the 'inner real me', was my soul, and it could have chosen another body this lifetime. I remember being deeply grateful that my soul chose my healthy body, my family, in this particular country, and at this time in history. I felt a sense of vastness, and an inexplicable knowing, that I had had many lifetimes, each with a soul's purpose. I was aware of thinking that these thoughts were strange, yet somehow true, and yet this was not a topic that was ever discussed in church or at home.

I felt the energy running through me become an intense White Light, which seemed connected to a higher spiritual dimension. I asked, 'What is my purpose in this lifetime?' A calm, clear inner voice replied: 'I was/am here to help communicate unusual and God-ideas to large numbers of people!' I only shared that treasured message with a few close friends. It sounded exciting and throughout my careers in media and energy work, I've often felt I was in the right place at the right time, helping to convey inspiring and healing ideas to the world at large.

I ventured into energy healing, seemingly by accident, when I was 11 years old, and my best friend, who knew I had some mystical, psychic connections, asked me 'to do something' for her father who was in the hospital. I closed my eyes and imagined bringing in certain colors of light into his hospital room. I did this for about 10 minutes. The next day she told me he was much improved and asked me what I did. I told her that while I had never done this before, I was guided to bring in and surround his body with certain colors. I described the details of his hospital room, as I saw them in my 'mind's eye.'

She and I were both completely stunned to learn that I had described her father's hospital room to the smallest detail! In that moment, I learned that I had an ability to cross into an unseen dimension! After that, I used color healing on sick pets and family members.

Years later, when I lived in Los Angeles, and was working in television and practicing Reiki, I went to a gathering and met a celebrated psychic who was reputed to channel Isis, the Egyptian Goddess of Life, and he gave me some fascinating insight. He said that I had been a healer over many lifetimes, and a number of them were spent as an energy healer in Isis's temple in Egypt, where we used to do a lot of color healing! I sensed that was how that ability manifested in this incarnation! This awareness of past lives has also enabled me to work more effectively with clients who have some unexplained ability or issue. I find that strong abilities, feelings, and/or phobias are likely manifestations from earlier lifetimes.

Los Angeles was especially serendipitous for me, and where I met my gifted husband Ron Lavin. At the time, Los Angeles was certainly one of the 'new age' centers of the country and I was hungry to experience shamanic trainings and the plethora of 'new age' workshops. Later, in New York, when I worked as a producer for Geraldo Rivera on his daily talk show, I was given the freedom to present many of these cutting-edge topics to the national audience. Over the seven years, I found inspiring experts and compelling personal stories and shared this bouquet of riches with our daily national audience. I produced programs on meditation, holistic medicine, energy healing, mental imagery, angelic encounters, reincarnation, fire walking, using one's mind to do spoon-bending, and many more subjects. Luminaries such as Dr. Deepak Chopra became frequent guests.

While there, opportunities to use energy healing continued to unfold. One day, a young nervous guest had a sudden nosebleed. I asked him to close his eyes and relax, and I 'turned on my hands' and sent him some healing energy, and he was fine a few minutes later. Another occasion occurred on the Long Island Railroad on my way to work from Long Beach into Manhattan. I was late and missed my earlier train, but I tuned in and felt for some reason, it was all right. After I sat down on the train seat I noticed that I felt a connection to a man sitting in the seat directly in front of me. After the train pulled out of the station, the man suddenly began thrashing around and frothing at the mouth, in what looked like an epileptic fit. I closed my eyes and 'turned on my hands' and again, just ran the energy into his chest and he calmed down within a minute. I kept my hands on his body, until the medics arrived at the next station. I was deeply grateful that the energy work I had learned enabled me to help this man.

Through the years as I continued on my dual purpose of working in media and energy healing, I have found that working as a One Light Healing Touch Practitioner and Instructor brings me a profound connection to my soul purpose. I believe that all our lives become part of the rich tapestry of life, and over time a pattern emerges. We all have the conscious choice to make our own strand strong, shimmering with light, and connected to others, helping others, as they help us. Let your light shine!

You are a most enlightened producer in this and related fields, and your work is so formative to helping the new paradigm emerge. – Beverly Rubik, Ph.D., Institute of Frontier Science

I saw on a daily basis her boundless energy and amazing creativity. Her ability to organize all her knowledge and ideas into one coherent program is legendary. — Steve North, veteran broadcast and print journalist

Printed in the United States
By Bookmasters